MW00744001

ANY
QUESTIONS?

Answers for Basic Investing

Dan Geffre

Any Questions? offers the answers that every investor must know about how to build real wealth ... in a format that's direct and easy to read.

Here's information that simplifies the investment process, outlines how the nation's economy impacts you, and helps you understand the wide variety of investments available to help you achieve all your financial goals.

- ✔ Certificates of Deposit
- ✔ Stocks and Bonds
- ✔ Mutual Funds
- ✔ Individual Retirement Accounts
- ✔ Annuities, Risk and More!

Any Questions? delivers.
It answers the real questions investors ask:

"How do I find a financial advisor I can trust?"

"Can I lose my money?"

"Which investments are right for me?"

"How do I get started?"

What investment students have to say about author and financial advisor Dan Geffre ...

"Dan makes investing interesting and fun. He helped me realize the many investments from which I can choose."

"Excellent overview of the subject of investing! Dan broadened my ideas on how to better utilize my assets."

"Dan's examples are easy to understand. He makes me feel good about learning."

To Ruth and Adrian, my mother and father,
whose support and sacrifices
I will never forget

Information and figures quoted in this book are believed reliable, but are not guaranteed. The data and opinions are for information only. While great care has been taken to insure accurate and current data, the ideas, principles, conclusions, and general suggestions contained in this book are subject to the laws and regulations of local, state and federal authorities, as well as to court cases and any revisions of court cases. The reader is thus urged to consult legal counsel regarding any points of law — this publication should not be used as a substitute for competent legal advice. If legal, financial or tax advice or other expert assistance is required, the services of a competent professional should be sought.

I.S.B.N. 0-9651517-0-0

First printing 1993
Second printing 1994
Third printing 1996

Any Questions?
P.O. Box 9872
Fargo, N.D. 58106–9872

Printed in U.S.A.

Table of Contents

Preface

Investing — especially for the first time — can be very uncomfortable. I know. I've been there. Feelings of anxiety are normal when it comes to investing your hard-earned money. These feelings can sometimes cloud your decision-making and keep you from investing for your future needs.

Feelings of apprehension are perfectly normal, especially for the first time investor. Do not feel alone. They should not, however, stop the average person from investing his or her money. The cost of living is going up year after year and you must deal with that reality. So what can you do?

In my opinion, the best way to eliminate these feelings of apprehension is to work with a financial consultant you can trust. Even after educating yourself, it may be difficult for you to know everything you need to know about investing to feel totally confident about your decisions. Things change in today's world. Unless you have instant access to financial information, it is difficult to react to those changes.

It is important, however, to have a general understanding of your investments. That general understanding, coupled with a working relationship with a trusted financial consultant, should be just the recipe for you to tackle those sometimes-uncomfortable decisions.

While there are no perfect answers for everyone on the best type of investments or investing, I have set out to provide you — the average conservative investor — with a guide that can help you understand the fundamentals of investing.

Many good books have been written on investing. While I could recommend these books to my clients, students and friends, they all seem to carry "extra" baggage. So I've written this introduction to investing to deal directly with what the average investor wants to know: the basics without all the extra baggage.

This book is directed to all levels of financial experience and all ages. No question is too basic when it comes to money. I hope you enjoy the reading.

Chapter 1: Introduction To Investing

For many investors, the 1990s will present serious financial challenges. They include one that most of us have not faced for years — the danger that lower interest rates will make it difficult for investors to find comparable yields and maintain their investment income when their fixed-income investments, like CDs and bonds, mature.

Looking back, the 1980s were a decade of remarkable economic contrasts. On one hand, the U.S. economy experienced the longest period of growth in its history. The stock market averaged 17.55% per year, as measured by the Standard & Poor's 500 index. The bond market also turned in a superior performance compared to historical norms, with an average yield of 10.33%. Inflation fell from 12% in 1980 to just 4.6% by the decade's end.

On the other hand, the 1980s will be remembered as the decade of explosive and, some would say, irresponsible debt growth. Leveraged buy-outs, junk bonds and speculation in commercial real estate characterized the period. In addition, the 1980s were the decade of the "yuppies" — members of the baby boom generation who were noted for their free-wheeling spending and unrestrained materialism.

Despite these contrasts (or perhaps because of them), the 1990s are turning out to be very different from the '80s. Debt has been repudiated by both businesses and individuals. And, as the baby boomers have children of their own, materialism is giving way to a more family-oriented lifestyle in which saving for the future is once again a priority.

These demographic, economic and market forces are

creating fundamental differences in the financial climate of the 1990s. We are on the verge of a new economic environment. Economic influences such as increased savings rates and less demand for debt will have significant implications for inflation, interest rates and investments.

To a large extent, the tremendous growth of debt since the mid-1950s was fueled by high rates of inflation. Both consumers and businesses realized that they could borrow money and pay it back later in depreciated dollars. People borrowed to build houses; companies borrowed to expand capacity; and over time we created ever-increasing debt loads.

However, in the 1980s, back-to-back recessions and other factors began to unwind inflation. The total debt growth of the private sector peaked in 1986, and has been rising at lower rates since.

As a result, the economic climate of the 1990s may be one of lower inflation, slower debt growth and lower interest rates than that of the 1980s. For many, this forecast is good news. For example, lower mortgage rates make homes more affordable. Lower inflation preserves the purchasing power of assets and fixed incomes during retirement.

For some investors, however, these conditions will present the very real danger of *reinvestment risk.* Income-oriented investors who became accustomed to cash investments such as CDs, Treasury bills and money funds yielding between 8% and 9% or more in the 1980s may not be able to find comparable yields when their investments mature in the 1990s. For example, investors who earned $40,000 in their investment income from CDs yielding 8% or 9% will not be able to find comparable yields when their CDs mature. When they reinvest, the lower-yielding CDs may be able to generate only approximately $25,000 of income. *Reinvestment risk may be the single greatest financial challenge of the 1990s.*

In fact, in the 1980s, "cash equivalent" investments such as CDs and money market funds earned an average of $4\frac{1}{2}\%$ more than the rate of inflation. Historically, these same investments have generally earned just $1\frac{1}{2}\%$ to 2% above the rate of inflation. The 1980s were an aberration. The 1990s should see a return to more normal real rates of return (Yield minus Inflation) on cash equivalent investments.

What should you do? I hope that by the end of this book you will have gained some general guidelines to follow to help you make informed investment decisions. Investing in the '90s will be very different from investing in the '80s. New challenges such as reinvestment risk require all investors to reevaluate their investments and make whatever changes are necessary to position their money for a new economic environment.

Why People Fail Financially

There are a number of reasons why people fail to become financially independent or fail to increase their standard of living. We all have choices in what we do with our money. Some choose to invest only in CDs; others choose stocks, bonds or other investments. Ultimately, the goal of every investor should be to develop a diversified investment plan that combines the safety of income with the rewards of growth.

The reason people fail financially is simply a lack of information. I am convinced that if investors knew more about investing and its history, nearly everyone would own more than just one type of investment. Most everyone would own a diversified portfolio of stocks, bonds and cash. Following are some reasons why I believe most people don't invest their money to their best advantage.

Procrastination

A secure retirement is unfortunately the least of most young people's worries. When we are young, we are more concerned with buying a bigger house or getting a more expensive car. Thoughts of retirement are far away. They bear little relationship to current needs and even less to future needs.

People near or in retirement often feel it's too late to start investing. They haven't yet realized that people are living a lot longer today than once was expected, and that inflation cares not whether you're in retirement or in your teens. It is going to eat away at the purchasing power of your money. One might even go as far as to say that how you invest your money at and during retirement is as important as during your working years!

Once you've reached retirement, it's very important that you have your money hedged against inflation, because you have no earning power left. *It's never too late to start!*

Lack of Understanding about Money

One reason many people own CDs is that they understand how they work. One big reason why people don't own a diversified portfolio is because of a lack of understanding of how different types of investments work. When you don't understand something, you tend to avoid it. However, after becoming more knowledgeable on how investments work, I am certain you will feel confident enough to invest your money wisely.

I am confident that if you learn how investments work and learn to apply the basic rules of investing, your standard of living will increase year after year.

Failure to Establish a Goal

One of the biggest attributes of successful people is their ability to set a goal and maintain a system to reach that goal. Without setting a goal, you won't have a realistic idea where you are headed and whether or not you will achieve your financial dreams.

If you want a secure retirement, you need to know exactly how much money you are going to need to maintain a standard of living you desire. To reach that goal, you are going to have to plan ahead to reap the rewards of working all your life.

Success in money management doesn't just come to some and not to others because of fate, chance or luck. Success can be predicted if you have a plan and faithfully follow it. But you need to set those goals and stick with them! Start today! Time is your greatest ally. It doesn't matter if you're 25, 45 or 65 years or older, you have money to work with. Invest it wisely!

Failure to Learn and Apply our Tax Laws

Along with death and inflation, taxes are certain to be with us. Tax laws are constantly changing and it's important to keep abreast of those changes.

The concept of *after-tax return* is overlooked by a majority of people. Taxes can significantly affect your returns and, subsequently, the size of your future estate. Proper tax planning will make a significant difference in your standard of living in the future.

Remember, *it's not what you make, it's what you keep!* A good financial consultant will be able to position your money to effectively deal with the effects of taxes on your real rate of return.

Don't Know a Financial Consultant to Trust

In my opinion, the single largest reason why people fail financially is they don't know anyone they can trust with their money. Unless you have a lot of time and resources, it is important to find a financial consultant to help guide you to financial success. I really believe that if more people knew a *qualified* financial consultant, who had their best interests at heart, most would invest their money profitably.

Without *your taking the initiative* to find someone who can help you, the chances of coming across a financial consultant who can do a good, honest job for you may be slim. Later in the book, I will give you directions on how to find the financial consultant who can help you reach financial independence.

Formula for Financial Success

Take a Long-Term Perspective

Investors who take a long-term perspective — a minimum of five years or even longer — are consistently the market's best performers. They may also get more sleep than do most short-term investors. In the short term, perhaps six months to two years, you cannot be sure of any return.

The 500-point single-day drop in the Dow Jones Industrial Average on October 19, 1987, did not provoke another Great Depression. The total decline during the October 1987 market crash erased only one year's gain in the Dow. The Dow actually ended 1987 with an overall gain, not a loss. Unchanged twelve-month stock market returns aren't that uncommon, yet few people remembered this fact during the 1987 post-crash hysteria. If you rode out the 1987 fluctuations, a properly diversified portfolio rewarded you for your patience and long-term perspective.

Investing for the long-term will usually reward you with greater returns on your investments and with a better night's sleep. Don't get discouraged if your investments haven't knocked your socks off in the short run. If you've invested your money in a diversified portfolio with a proven track record, you will do just fine in the years ahead.

Develop a System of Investing

Once you decide to build a diversified portfolio of cash, income and growth investments, you are going to need a strategy to reach proper diversification. Moreover, you are going to need a way to adjust your portfolio to take advantage of the constantly changing markets.

To monitor your portfolio, you will need a *system* to keep you on the road to success. Your system should include a systematic way to reposition your money based on current conditions. For example, if the stock market rose substantially for two straight years, you might be overweighted in the growth investments area. How will you — and your portfolio — adjust to the inflated values in the growth portion of your portfolio?

A system will make the proper adjustments so you will avoid being overweighted in any one area at any given time. It should be able to give you a perspective of how you're doing in terms of each of your individual investments, as well as a bird's-eye view of the portfolio's total return. Many people don't know exactly how well their investments have done in the last 12 months. Subsequently, they don't have a realistic perspective on how well their investments are performing relative to what they should be doing. A system will show you exactly how well (or how poorly) each of your investments is doing at any given time.

Finally, and most importantly, a system will keep you on track in reaching your goals. You need a reporting system to show you where you are, so you don't get sidetracked along the way.

Proper Diversification and Asset Allocation

Once again, it pays to follow this most basic and time-honored investment truism. All too many people have too much of their money invested in one or two types of investments. This can be a recipe for disaster if your group of particular investments falters badly.

If you have allocated your money so it can take advantage of current investment opportunities, you are on the right track to successful investing. It is not wise to put all your eggs in one basket. But that's what most people have done by buying only CDs or stocks. Proper diversification, among a number of different investments, will help provide you with *consistent returns* year after year. It will help keep your portfolio from experiencing large fluctuations as the investment markets work through their cycles.

Diversification and asset allocation reduce the risks within your portfolio. By spreading out your money, you are not subjecting your account to any undue risks associated with any one particular market at any given time.

For example, look at the risk many portfolios have experienced by being heavily invested in the fixed-income area. Portfolios heavily weighted in CDs in 1992 and 1993 suffered severe losses. Interest rates have dropped and the portfolio's income is down 50% or more from previous years.

Proper diversification and asset allocation helps prevent major losses and gives you consistent returns year after year.

Buy Quality

The market often can be driven by rumors and unfounded fears. It is very important that you own higher quality investments in a fluctuating market. The higher quality securities will have more staying power if market conditions do continue to decline. Moreover, in a down market, high quality investments tend to recover more quickly than lower-rated securities.

Money

To become financially independent, you must save regularly and make your money grow. Especially if you begin when you are young, not a lot of money is necessary to build a substantial estate ... if you know how to save and invest properly. Allow the magic of compounding to do its thing. The investors who create the largest estates are those who invest money from every paycheck, come rain or shine.

One of the most important keys to financial success is to *live beneath your means*. It is imperative that you spend less than you earn! Cutting back on expenses, increasing your savings and adding to your investments are the only route to take to enjoy a secure standard of living throughout your working and retirement years.

Educate Yourself

You must have at least a general understanding of how your investments work. *Never* invest in anything that you don't understand. Of course, you can't be expected to know everything about your investments (that's the financial consultant's responsibility), but you should have a general knowledge of how they work.

An easy way to educate yourself is by taking investment classes offered through Community or Adult Education. These classes are normally offered through the public school systems. They are usually taught in the evenings and can be an objective way to get information. Adult education classes also allow you the opportunity to ask questions.

Another way to increase your knowledge is by reading. There are a number of good books available that cover the basics of investing. You can get these books at book stores and libraries.

Finally, your financial consultant can provide you with a basic explanation of how your investments work. Developing a relationship with a financial consultant whom you trust can be a tremendous source of help and information.

Chapter 2: Economics Understanding the Economy

The performance of an investment will be influenced by the economy. It is much easier, for example, to pick a good stock in a good market than it is to pick a good stock in a falling market. In addition, it is usually difficult to get an accurate reading of exactly where the economy is today!

Conflicting reports are frequently issued, giving analysts different readings and interpretations of the direction our economy is headed. There are almost as many economic theories as there are economists. That's why it is so important to be diversified at all times. No one has been 100% accurate predicting our economic health over the years.

The *general direction* of the economy can be helpful for us to formulate an investment strategy that will take advantage of present investment opportunities. Let's take a look at who controls the health of our economy.

The Forces that Control our Economy

There are three basic forces that control the health of our economy. It is important to understand how these three forces affect economic activity: the government, the Federal Reserve and foreign investors, all in different ways.

The Government
Think back to a time when your taxes were raised. What effect did those additional taxes have on your spending? I can probably guess. They most likely slowed your spending habits because you had less disposable income.

Fiscal policy is the government's use of taxation and

expenditure programs to maintain a stable, growing economy. If the economy is in a recession, the government can choose to increase its own spending to stimulate demand and create jobs. Additionally, the government can choose to cut certain taxes which will increase consumers' disposable income, and thus create demand.

One area where the government can spend money is by increasing spending for public works. Such programs can help stimulate the economy by creating new jobs, and thus more spending by those hired for those jobs. Welfare transfer payments can also be controlled by the government as a further stimulating force. For example, in particularly lean times, unemployment compensation can be prolonged.

If the government feels the economy is overheated, it can choose to increase taxes or decrease its own spending to slow down the economy. By raising or lowering taxes, the government has a tighter reign on disposable income and thus the level of spending and consumption by consumers.

The government cannot simply try to control the level of economic activity with free reigns. Just like the rest of us, the government has a budget (believe it or not) that needs to be taken into consideration when making taxing and spending decisions. When the government's spending equals its revenues collected, the government's budget is said to be *balanced.* When spending exceeds receipts, there is a budgetary *deficit* which increases the national debt.

If individuals continue to spend more money than they earn, eventually they will become bankrupt. Is the same fate a possibility for the federal government? For two principal reasons, the answer is "no."

The first point is that government debt need not be eliminated or reduced. When debt becomes due, the government typically issues new debt to pay off existing maturing debt. Second, the government has control over the printing presses. The government has the power to create more money to pay the principal and interest on debt. However, if this power is abused, runaway inflation will surely be the result.

The only portion of the debt that many economists regard as troublesome is the amount held by foreign investors, because payment of that portion represents the transfer of funds out of the American economy.

The important thing to remember is that the government's use of its own spending and taxation directly affects our personal spending habits and thus, the direction of economic activity.

The Federal Reserve

The Federal Reserve System was established by the Federal Reserve Act of 1913 to regulate the U.S. monetary and banking system. The Fed is comprised of twelve regional banks that are part of the system. Its origins go back to 1907, when a sudden nationwide financial scare resulted in a disastrous run on the banks. J.P. Morgan saved the day by importing $100 million worth of gold from Europe. The government decided it couldn't continue to rely on industry giants to save the economy. That resulted in the establishment of this powerful banking system.

The Federal Reserve System's main functions are to regulate the nation's banking system and control the nation's money supply. Although the members of the system's governing board are appointed by the President of the United States and confirmed by the Senate, the Fed is considered an independent entity; that status is supposed to keep its decision-making free of political influence.

The Fed accomplishes its objectives through monetary supply. Monetary policy attempts to control the supply of money and credit in the economy. This will affect interest rates causing an increase or decrease in economic activity. The Fed's top priority is to control inflation.

Generally, if the Fed is expanding the money supply (putting more money into the economy), interest rates go down. There is "easy money;" that is, credit is easier to obtain and at lower interest rates. This will allow consumers to go out and borrow money at low rates, thus increasing their spending, which in turn increases economic activity.

The opposite is true if the Fed contracts the money supply (takes money out of the economy). When the Fed takes money out of the economy, interest rates rise and the amount of credit tightens up because there is less money to lend. The banks loaning out the money demand a higher interest rate, and consumers slow down spending because of the higher cost of borrowing. This causes economic activity to slow down.

The Fed regulates the money supply by buying and selling U.S. government securities in the open market. When it buys securities, the Fed injects money into the banking system, allowing banks to lend more money and increase the money supply. The opposite is true for the selling of securities.

Second, the Fed regulates reserve requirements for the banks. If the reserve requirement goes up, the percentage of deposits at the bank that can be lent out goes down, thereby reducing money supply.

In general, as the Fed puts more money into the economy, interest rates fall and consumers borrow and spend more. When the Fed takes money out of the economy, it becomes more scarce and banks charge a higher rate of interest to borrow. Consumers spend less, slowing down the economy.

Like the government, the Federal Reserve must be careful how much money it puts into or takes out of the economy. If the Fed puts too much money in the economy, it can lead to inflation and higher interest rates. If the Fed puts too little money into the economy, it can lead to a recession. The Fed's job is to put just enough money into the economy to keep it going - without inflation.

Throughout most of history, the Federal Reserve and the government have done a pretty good job keeping the economy running smoothly ... except for the late 1970s. They won't soon forget that period, and have in fact vowed not to repeat.

Everyone Else in the World

The third big influence on our economy is *everyone else in the world!* Because our country has run up huge budget deficits over the years, we are dependent on foreigners to buy our debt. Foreigners have used their money to buy our Treasury bills, notes and bonds that help finance our government's debt. Because of our reliance on them, our interest rates must remain high enough for these investors to remain interested in buying our debt. If foreigners didn't loan us their money, we would be forced to raise our own interest rates higher to attract other investors.

Additionally, how much we buy from foreigners and how

much they purchase from us partially determines the direction of our economy. If the rest of the world decides that there are better values in different countries, they can choose to buy the cheaper goods elsewhere. Foreign spending for American products will slow down, and profitability will decline in our economy. Ours is a global economy! What we do and what other countries do to us directly affects the direction of all our economies.

Clearly, the government, the Fed and foreigners impact the direction of our economy. It is important to look for general trends so that we can take advantage of opportunities as they arise.

The U.S. economy is watched by legions of economic analysts, corporations, and other pundits. These analysts look at a variety of economic indicators to assess how the economy is faring and where it is headed. Since these figures are constantly in the news, understanding what they mean and how they affect you is important.

Measuring the Health of the Economy

To help us keep track of the economy and its health, economic indicators are issued periodically by the government. These indicators give us an idea of the direction in which economic activity is moving. Unfortunately, these signs will not give us a black and white picture of exactly how our economy is doing. Not only do economists interpret the data differently, but different parts of the economy will grow or slow down at the same time, giving us a conflicting picture. Still, it is important to keep an eye on the economic indicators so we can be aware of potential changes in the economy.

One of the most significant barometers of the economic health of our country used by most analysts is the *Gross Domestic Product* (GDP). GDP is the total value of goods and services produced in the U.S. economy over a time period, normally one year.

The GDP growth rate is the primary indicator of the status of the economy. It is made up of consumer and government purchases, private domestic and foreign investments in the

U.S., and the total value of exports. The figures for GDP on an annual basis are released every quarter by the government. A recession occurs when Real GDP (Gross Domestic Product adjusted for inflation) has declined for two successive quarters. If the GDP is considerably higher than in previous years, the economy is growing rapidly.

Another widely watched indicator is the *index of leading economic indicators*, released monthly and adjusted for inflation. The twelve indicators that make up the index are compiled by the U.S. government and include hours being worked by factory workers, new claims for unemployment insurance, changes in inventory, new building permits, and other indicators. These indicators tend to forecast future trends in the economy and are widely watched.

The index of leading economic indicators is considered a *leading* indicator of the economy. It will precede the upward and downward movement of the economy.

Another trend watched by analysts is the *lagging* indicators — those which give us a picture of past developments. The *unemployment report,* issued on the first Friday of every month, is considered a lagging indicator. The unemployment report gives us a reading of how many recently unemployed people are searching for a job. However, this report can give us a misleading picture. The unemployment rate may go up because people have grown more hopeful about finding a job and have resumed their search. It does not count those who have simply given up looking for employment.

A better indicator of the economy may be the *payroll employment figure.* This indicator counts the number of employees currently working for companies around the country. As this figure rises, so might consumer spending, and along with it, the economy and stock market.

Inflation is probably the biggest concern of everybody. It can be measured a number of ways. One is the *Consumer Price Index* (CPI). The CPI, also known as the *cost of living index*, is based on the costs of housing, food, transportation and electricity. It tracks the changes in the prices of its components. If the CPI is rising, then it can be said that inflation is on the rise. Many pension and employment contracts are tied to changes in consumer prices as protection against inflation and reduced purchasing power.

Another inflation indicator is the *producer price index* (PPI). The producer price index gauges the change in wholesale prices. Prices are calculated as products move through the manufacturing process, before they reach the consumer. It was formerlly called the *wholesale price index.* An increase in PPI might suggest that price increases will soon be passed on to the consumer in the form of higher consumer prices resulting in a rise in inflation.

Housing starts indicate how well off consumers consider themselves. When consumers feel financially secure, they take out loans to realize the American dream of home owner-ship. Therefore, trends in housing starts can indicate overall consumer confidence.

There are many other indicators that monitor the health of the economy. We, as investors, don't have enough time or expertise to make heads or tails of many of them. A general feel for the direction of the economy, however, will help give you a broad direction to pursue as your portfolio of invest-ments grows over time.

Chapter 3: Income Investments

Income investments are simply investments that pay you interest, or income, on a periodic schedule for the use of your money. Unlike growth investments, which may not offer a predictable future rate of return, income investments offer the stability of knowing exactly how much interest you will receive until your investment matures. If you hold the income investment until maturity, you will know exactly what your rate of return will be.

One of the most popular types of income investments is Certificates of Deposit (CDs). Other popular income alternatives range from government, corporate and municipal bonds to the more risky junk bonds. Let's start with the simplest of income investments.

Passbook Savings

Passbook savings is an account that can be opened at banks with a typical minimum of $100 or less. Interest earned on this type of account is typically the lowest rate offered. The bank's expenses are higher because you have access to your money at any time. This money is insured by the FDIC.

Money Market Accounts

Money market accounts have become very popular in recent times. A money market account may be described as a combined savings and checking account giving you the advantage of both. There are two basic types of money market accounts: the *bank money market deposit account* and the *money market mutual fund.*

Bank Money Market Deposit Accounts

Money market deposit accounts at banks or savings and loan associations yield just slightly less than ordinary money market mutual funds. The reason is that banks and S&Ls costs are higher with this type of account because of transactions costs and associated overhead.

If you feel you would like to earn more than the passbook savings account is paying and still keep your money safe, ask your bank about its insured money market account rate. It may and probably will be a little higher than the passbook savings.

Money market deposit accounts generally pay competitive rates to short–term CDs. You have access to all of your money at any time by writing a check on your account. To prevent you from using this type of an account as an interest–bearing checking account, the bank may limit the number of checks that can be written per month, generally a maximum of three. There is no penalty for withdrawals.

A money market deposit account is a good place to store temporary cash or emergency money because it always pays the current market interest rate. If rates are rising, the interest rate in your money market deposit account will also rise. Conversely, if the prevailing interest rates are falling, the rate earned on your money market will also fall. Most financial institutions change their rates weekly after watching the Treasury auctions to see which direction interest rates have moved.

Money Market Mutual Fund

Money market mutual funds look and act like the bank money market deposit accounts. However, there are big differences between the two from the standpoint of how they are put together.

The bank money market account is a simple account that is nothing more than a savings account with check-writing privileges. The money market mutual fund however, is structured as a mutual fund. It is designed to purchase short-term money market instruments and pass on the higher interest rates to investors whose savings might not otherwise earn competitive rates.

The money market funds combine investors' money to earn the higher rates on Jumbo CDs or to buy commercial paper or Treasuries or other short-term bank paper. This is why money market mutual funds pay a slightly higher rate of return than the bank money market deposit accounts. In effect, the funds make short term loans to federal, state, and local governments as well as to corporations and U.S. and foreign banks.

Money market mutual funds are required to have maturities of 90 days or less for the entire investment portfolio. When the money managers of the portfolio think interest rates are about to move lower, they will extend the maturities of the short-term "paper" closer to the maximum 90 days. If, however, they think interest rates are about to move up, they will only extend their maturities out a couple of days.

Unlike bank money market deposit accounts whose interest rate changes weekly, the money market mutual fund's rate changes daily. Because of the daily rate change, you can't predict exactly how much interest you'll receive during a given period.

Money market mutual funds are not covered by federal deposit insurance. But the government requires that 95% of the funds assets receive the highest rating from at least two investment rating agencies. For the ultraconservative investor, there are funds that specialize in investing in only the safest of short-term money market instruments such as Treasury bills.

One of the biggest attractions of a money market mutual fund is its liquidity. You can have access to your money at any time by writing a check on your account. Money market mutual funds can offer unlimited check-writing privileges for any amount per check, while others may require a minimum of $100 per check. You can use this account as a temporary holding place for cash or emergency money, or use it to pay bills such as income taxes. Money market mutual funds may charge a fee for the check writing privileges. Their annual fee can range anywhere from $0 to $100.

There are basically two types of money market mutual

funds: taxable and tax–free. With taxable funds, you pay federal and state taxes on your savings as you would on any type of savings account. The earnings are taxable because the investments within the fund are taxable such as CDs, Treasuries, and short-term paper.

With the tax–free money market account, your earnings are subject to state but *not* federal taxes. The earnings are free of federal taxes because the fund's investments include short-term municipal paper, not taxable investments such as CDs. The earnings are state taxable because generally, these money market mutual funds hold the short-term paper from municipalities scattered around the U.S. and are not domiciled in your own state.

Certificates of Deposit

Certificates of deposit are one of the most widely used forms of savings today. Many savers prefer to lock up their money for a fixed period of time at a fixed rate. These CD maturities range anywhere from just a few months to as long as 10 years.

Depending on the current market interest rates, it may make more sense to extend or shorten your maturities. If you expect rates to be rising in the near future, a shorter-term maturity strategy might make sense. If however, rates are abnormally high like in the early 1980s, it would make sense to extend the maturities of your CDs to lock in the high interest rates.

CDs are a loan to a bank in exchange for a rate of return called *interest*. The bank then uses the money it borrowed from you and reloans it to businesses and consumers who need to borrow money to buy homes, cars, appliances and other things.

Interest can be offered two ways. Some banks advertise *compound interest*; others offer *simple interest*. You should always check whether the bank or savings institution will pay you simple or compound interest.

The yield on a simple-interest CD is much lower than you might expect. For example let's say you bought a $1,000 five-year simple-interest certificate of deposit paying 6%. It would pay you $60 interest every year, totalling $300 for the five-year term. On the other hand, if the five-year CD were paying 6% compounded interest, you would end up with about $347 of interest for the five-year period.

If the CD is paying simple interest, that means the interest will not earn interest. Over a long period of time, compounding (interest earning interest) can make a big difference in how your money grows.

Be sure to check what the bank's penalties are for early withdrawal. Many banks may tack on stiff penalties to discourage early withdrawals. Others may offer lesser penalties as a feature of their CDs. They do this to attract new investors.

You may also want to find out how you will be notified when your CD is about to mature and how much time you have to make a decision on whether to withdraw or redeposit the money. The banks generally send you a reminder ten days to two weeks before you have to make that decision.

If you've collected over $100,000 in savings, you may be able to earn more interest than the average CD buyer who has less than $100,000. If you have at least $100,000 you would then be able to purchase a *Jumbo* CD. These Jumbo CDs can pay up to as much as 1% more than regular CDs because the bank's costs are less when it accepts larger amounts of money.

One cautionary note concerning Jumbo CDs: Banks will only insure money up to the $100,000 limit in your name. You might want to move part of your money to another financial institution if you need to have all your money insured all the time.

You may be able to get a little higher interest rate by putting your money into a certificate of deposit at a brokerage house instead of a bank. Brokered CDs also have the backing of the Federal Deposit Insurance Corporation (FDIC). The reason the rates are generally higher for the brokered CDs is that many brokerage firms buy small-denomination CDs in bulk from banks. The brokerage firms can also choose from a wide variety of banks across the U.S. whose rates might be slightly higher than those offered locally. After the brokerages buy the CDs, they then offer the certificates to the public in $1,000 units.

Brokered CDs do not pay compound interest. The interest earned is generally moved to a money market fund which is typically paying less than the CD. Brokered CDs may allow you to sell early without suffering an early withdrawal penalty. Generally you will not be charged a commission for buying or selling your CD at the brokerage firm. The broker is either paid a fee by the bank, or takes a bit of yield as his or her fee.

Brokered CDs can trade like bonds. If interest rates fall after you've bought your CD and you need to cash it in at that time, you may be able to sell at a profit plus earn interest up to the day you sell the CD. On the other hand, if interest rates rise after you buy a CD, your certificate value may fall and you may get less than you invested.

Treasury Securities

Treasury securities are the means by which the U.S. government borrows money. Because the government's expenditures regularly exceed tax and other revenues by staggering sums, they offer three basic types of debt; *Treasury bills, notes, and bonds.* These bills, notes, and bonds are interest-paying IOUs from the government so they have money to run their daily operations. Because the government must borrow money when its tax receipts don't cover its expenditures, they frequently sell both short-and long-term securities.

Treasury bills are sold in minimum denominations of $10,000 and they come in three-, six- and twelve-month maturities. These bills have the shortest term of the Treasury securities. Unlike longer-term debt securities, they carry no coupon rate of interest. Instead, they are sold at a discount. Treasury bills are issued on a discount basis under competitive bidding, with the face amount paid to you at maturity.

If you want to tie up your money for a longer period of time than one year, perhaps *Treasury notes* might be an option for your investment money. Treasury notes are sold in minimum denominations of $5,000 when they have maturities of less than five years — and in minimums of $1,000 when they have maturities of five and ten years. Interest earned with these notes is payable every six months. They can be sold prior to maturity but the price you receive is subject to market conditions (fluctuation).

Treasury bonds also sell in minimums of $1,000 but have maturities ranging from more than ten years all the way to thirty years. Because the maturity of Treasury bonds is longer, you assume more interest rate risk and consequently you will receive a generally higher interest rate than bills or notes. The risk to you is in tying up your money for a long time at a fixed rate. If interest rates rise in the future, you will be tied to the low interest rate bonds or forced to sell at a loss if you needed your money when rates were higher.

Treasury securities come to the market at different times. Three- and six-month bills are auctioned every Monday. Twelve-month bills are sold every fourth Thursday. Treasury notes with maturities of two and five years are generally sold at the end of each month. Three-year and ten-year notes are generally sold every three months: in February, May, August and November. The 30-year bond is offered twice a year, in February and August.

You can buy Treasury issues directly from the Federal Reserve or from one of its branch offices. You can also order them by mail, using forms that you get from your local Fed bank. You can also buy Treasuries from a commercial bank or your broker. This may eliminate much of the hassle of buying the bonds and filling out forms but the cost can range from $30 to $60 and will ultimately lower your rate of return.

One of the biggest advantages of owning Treasuries, is that the interest you earn is exempt from state and local taxes. Given all things the same, a Treasury will yield, after taxes, slightly more than a CD with the same maturity and interest rate.

Another big benefit of Treasuries is that there is no maximum for federal government protection like there is with the $100,000 FDIC insurance protection. You can put as much as you want into Treasuries and still keep the promise of backing from the federal government.

U.S. Savings Bonds

If you wish to have interest you receive deferred, or would like to make small gifts of government bonds, you may want to take a look at *Series* EE bonds. They require a lot less money to start than many of the other income investment options.

Series EE bonds work a little different than Treasury bonds. Instead of paying the face amount for the bond, you buy the bonds at a discount. For example, you pay $500 to purchase a $1,000 face amount bond. Because you've only paid $500 for a $1,000 bond, you've bought it at a discount. As time goes on, the interest you've earned will build up until, at some point down the road, the value of your EE bond reaches the face amount of $1,000.

Because the interest rate changes each May and October, there is no stated maturity. The lower the current interest rates, the longer it will take for your bond to reach face value. If, however, you hold your bond for at least five years, you're guaranteed 4%. So, at a minimum, your money will reach its face value in eighteen years. If you hold the bonds past maturity, they will continue earning the market interest rate for 30 years. If you decide to turn in your EE bonds in less than five years, for example six months, you are still assured a minimum return. The guaranteed rates are mere minimums. EE bond interest can rise with interest rates in general.

The interest you earn is exempt from state and local income taxes and personal property taxes. Federal taxes are deferred until you cash in the bonds. This means you can buy them several years before retirement and defer taxes until after you retire, when presumably you'll be in a lower tax bracket.

Series EE savings bonds can make a good savings alternative for people who want to lower their tax bill and save money to pay for their children's education. The Technical and Miscellaneous Revenue Act of 1988 (TAMRA) offers an exclusion of interest income on EE savings bonds issued after 1989.

If you use the redeemed principal and interest to pay for higher education tuition expenses during the year of redemption, the income is excluded from your gross income. The exclusion is available if you or your spouse are at least 24 years old at the time of purchase and don't have too high an income. The gross income figures are raised each year to adjust for inflation. In 1992 the phase out begins at incomes between $62,900 and $92,000 for couples and between $41,950 and $56,950 for single parents.

One of the nice features of the U.S. EE savings bonds is that you don't need a truckload of money to start an investment program. EE bonds denominations range from minimums of $25 to a maximum of $15,000 issue price ($30,000 face amount) in the name of any one person. EE bonds are eligible for exchange to Series HH bonds six months after issue but they must have a current redemption of at least $500.

If you've held your Series EE bonds for some time and now feel like you want to start taking the interest income in cash rather than deferring them in the EE bonds, you may want to consider exchanging them for *Series* HH bonds. These bonds pay interest every six months and all of the interest earned is taxable as current income except for the interest earned from the EE bonds will be deferred until the bond is sold.

The interest on HH bonds is not subject to state or local taxes but is subject to federal income taxes. EE bonds may be exchanged for HH bonds but the reverse doesn't hold true. The HH bonds are not exchangeable and should be redeemed as they reach final maturity. The interest is paid semi-annually at an annual rate of 4%; they mature ten years after you've purchased them.

U.S. savings bonds are guaranteed as the principal and interest by the full faith and credit of the U.S. government.

Bonds

Bonds once offered the fainthearted a safe harbor for their money with no excitement and minimal risk. At one time bonds were considered one of the safest investments available after CDs. Oh, how times have changed!

With the advent of excessively high inflation and interest rates in the early 1980s coupled with the junk bond debacle in the mid-1980s, bond prices have been rising and falling like a bronco with a burr under its saddle. Rates now fluctuate more in a day than they used to in a whole year. Because interest rates are changing dramatically, so are bond prices. Bond prices move in the opposite direction of interest rates. During the later part of the 1980s and early 1990s bond prices have fluctuated as much as stock prices.

Despite the uncertainties in the bond market, investors have gone on a bond buying binge. One must carefully weigh the risks associated with bonds. You should understand how bonds work before you become mesmerized by the promise of regular interest payments.

There are ways you can lose money even in the safest bonds. Buying a bond, throwing it in a drawer and forgetting it is very risky. You must keep an eye on your bonds much like you do with your stock investments. As stocks values can fall, so can the value of your bonds. They are both tied to the financial strength of the company backing them.

Bonds are IOUs by the issuer, promising to pay a set rate of interest and to repay your principal in a fixed period of time. They can be issued by the government, corporations or municipalities.

When you go to the bank to buy a CD, you are loaning your money to the bank who then takes that same money and uses it to finance its outgoing loans. The same is true of bonds. You give your money to the entity (corporation), and they agree to pay your money back in the future, including interest. They use your money to finance their operations. They may pay off other loans, buy more products, or use it to expand.

There are two basic types of bonds. You may hear a bond's interest referred to as its *coupon*. That's because some bond certificates come with detachable coupons, each one representing a scheduled interest payment. With these coupon bonds, you actually clip a coupon and send it in at the appropriate time to receive your interest payment. There aren't many *coupon bonds* outstanding anymore. The reason is simply that their method of interest collection is cumbersome and slow.

Bonds with coupons are called *bearer bonds* because they are assumed to belong to whomever possesses them. Today, however, most bonds are *registered* in the holder's name and have no coupons. With registered bonds, the issuer automatically sends the interest payments to the holder listed on its records.

How the Interest Rate Is Determined
On Income Investments

The *interest rate* offered by a bond issuer is determined by market forces such as the issuer's credit standing, the length of maturity, current interest rate conditions and call provisions. If the issuer has a lower credit rating because of poor business conditions or has a short track record of earnings and sales, it may have to offer a higher interest rate to attract money to compensate for additional risk. A financially secure company with the highest credit rating will pay less than a corporation with a lesser quality rating.

To compensate for locking up your money for intermediate and long-term maturities, issuers are forced to offer you higher interest rates than short-term maturities because of interest rate risk. In general, the longer the maturity date, the higher your rate of interest will be. For example, a one-year corporate bond will yield much less than a 20-year bond. The time you have to tie up your money is a perceived risk. To be compensated for committing our money for that long, we demand a higher rate of return.

When the Federal Reserve decides to tighten credit or raise interest rates to cool down the economy, for a short period of time, short-term rates may be temporarily higher than long-term rates, as borrowers scramble to obtain money. This condition is called an inverted yield curve.

Depending on the issuer, bond maturities can range anywhere from months to 40 years. Depending on the purpose of the funds, the issuer may offer short, intermediate, or long-term maturities.

Short-term maturities range from one to five years.

Intermediate maturities range from about five to ten years.

Long-term bonds have maturities of more than ten years from original issue, but terms of fifteen to twenty years are the most common.

How Bonds Work

It may be surprising to learn that bond prices fluctuate just as stock prices do. Bonds are priced differently than stocks, however. Bonds are priced with a face value of $1,000. So ten bonds would equal $10,000 worth of bonds. But, because bond prices fluctuate with interest rates, their current value may be different than the original $1,000 face value. Depending on current interest rates, bonds may be priced at *par, premium* or *discount.*

Par =	$1,000
Premium =	$1,000 +
Discount =	$1,000 -

When bonds are priced at the offering they are generally priced at *par* (100) or at $1,000 per bond. If the issuer needed to raise 10 million in capital, he would bring to the market 10,000 bonds offered at par (10,000 x $1,000 = $10 million). So if you were to buy some of these bonds at the offering you would pay par for the bond.

If a bond is selling at a price below its $1,000 face amount, it is said to be selling at a *discount.* Bonds sell at a discount when new bonds offering higher interest rates are issued, making the old low-rate bonds less attractive. So if a $1,000 bond is selling at a below-par price of 90 or 95, it now has a market value of only $900 or $950. You could buy ten of these bonds for $9,500 ($950 x 10).

If a bond is selling at a price above its $1,000 face amount, it is said to be selling at a *premium.* The reason bonds may sell for a premium, or more than $1,000 per bond, is that presumably the premium bond carries a higher interest rate than do current new bonds being offered. A premium bond may be priced at 105 for example. That means the bond is carrying a premium of $50 per $1,000 bond and has a current price of $1,050 per bond. If you were going to buy ten of these premium bonds, they would cost you $10,500 ($1,050 x 10).

Essentially what happens is that as interest rates and economic conditions change, so do the prices of bonds. They fluctuate during the life of the bond. At some time, the price of the bonds may be at a discount or a premium depending on the prevailing interest rates. If you hold your bonds until maturity, the issuer promises to pay back the par value of the bond.

When Interest Rates Rise, Bond Prices Fall; When Interest Rates Fall, Bond Prices Rise

Why?

Let's say you bought a bond at par ($1,000) and it was paying 7% interest. Then, one year later, interest rates started rising and the same kind of bond offered one year later was paying 8%. What would happen to your 7% bond? It would make it look less attractive because people can now earn a higher rate of interest (8%) than your current bond paying 7%. If you wanted to sell your 7% bond, you would get less than par because the bond is less attractive. If you sold it, depending on prevailing higher rates, you would get less than you put in, and you would be forced to sell at a discount.

Conversely, if interest rates fell a year later on your current 7% bond to 6%, your bond would become more valuable and you could then choose to sell the bond at a premium because of its attractive interest rate.

If you plan to hold your bond until maturity, it really doesn't matter where your bond trades during its life (as long as the issuer backing the bond doesn't go into default). Remember, you'll get par back at maturity. Only when you are forced to sell your bond before maturity do the premium or discount fluctuations become increasingly important.

Let me repeat: *If you hold your bond until maturity, the issuer promises to pay back par value for the bond.* Let's say you buy 10 premium bonds at a cost of 105 per bond. It would cost you $10,500 to own these bonds. If you held them to maturity, the issuer would pay you par for the bonds. So you would get back $10,000 plus interest during the life of the bond. Your $500 premium you paid for the bond would be amortized during the bonds life until, at maturity, the bond would be priced at par or 100.

You paid $10,500 and got back $10,000. Doesn't sound like too good of a deal does it? But the bonds were priced at a premium because they paid a higher rate of interest than the current bond offerings. Ultimately you earned more interest during the life of this bond than did others who bought the lower-interest-paying par bonds. The extra interest you earned made up for the $500 premium you lost. The bottom line is that you've earned about the same total return as bondholders buying bonds today at par, given everything else stays the same.

Conversely, if you paid 95 ($950 per bond) for 10 bonds, they would cost you $9,500. At maturity, the issuer would give you back par value or $10,000 plus interest earned during the life of the bond. You earned an extra $500 because of the discount price you paid. However, the reason the bonds may have been at a discount is that they paid a lower interest rate than current bonds. Even though you got an extra $500, you earned less interest during the life of the bond than did those who are now buying bonds at par with a higher interest rate. Given all things the same, your total return would be about the same.

Price movements can mean significant profits or losses to bond buyers. It is very important that you understand the risks associated with bonds *before* you buy any of these securities.

Yields

Naturally, as you consider bonds for your balanced portfolio, you need to know exactly what return you'll earn and when you get your money back. Unlike CDs, where you put in $10,000 and years later you get back your $10,000 plus interest, when you purchase a bond that has already been issued in the market, you may pay a premium ($10,500) or discount ($9,500) from the face value ($10,000) for your bond. Because of this, your *real* return may differ from the stated interest rate offered. The issuer doesn't care whether you paid a premium or a discount for the bond, they will only pay back par ($10,000) for the bonds. Let's look at 4 important types of yields: *coupon yield, current yield, yield to maturity, and yield to call.*

The *coupon yield* is the stated interest rate that the borrower promises to pay. This rate is stated on the certificate and is fixed for the life of the bond. It is expressed as an annual percentage of the bond's par value. For example, a $10,000 (par) bond that pays $800 interest annually has a coupon yield of 8% ($800/$10,000).

The *current yield* is the actual *income rate of return* you will receive if you hold the bond until maturity. This shows the relationship of the bond's coupon rate to its current price. For example, a $9,500 (discount) bond that has an 8% coupon ($800 interest per year) has a current yield of 8.4% ($800/$9,500).

The *yield to maturity* is the yield that gives you the bottom line. It is the most important concept of yield because it is the yield upon which all bond prices are based. It includes both interest earned and the appreciation to face value at maturity when the bonds are bought at a discount. It also takes into account the amortization to face value when bonds are bought at a premium. It essentially takes into account your loss of premium paid or gain of discount earned. It is the *actual rate of return* you will receive if you hold the bond until maturity.

The *yield to call* is equivalent to yield to maturity, except that it is calculated based on a particular optional call date and call price. You should look at the lower of yield to maturity and yield to call in projecting your potential return.

Bond Interest Rates

There are two basic ingredients which determine a bond's interest rate: *maturity and quality.*

Maturity is the length of time you are lending your money to the issuer. If you lend your money for 10 years, you are taking a different risk than if you lend it for one year. Short-term rates are generally lower than long-term rates. A one-year CD will pay a lower rate of interest than a 10 year CD. If you are willing to lend your money for a longer period of time, you will usually get a higher rate of interest because of potential economic changes in the future.

One exception to this rule: When the Federal Reserve

decides to restrict credit, short-term rates surge as borrowers scramble to obtain money. In this case the yield curve becomes inverted, and temporarily, short-term rates exceed the long-term interest rates. The purpose of the rise in short-term interest rates is to cool off the economy and help lower inflation. If the Fed keeps these short-term rates too high for too long, the result could lead to a recession.

The *quality* of the issuer also determines what it must pay to borrow your money. The issue here is simple. How certain are you that the issuer will pay you back with interest as scheduled?

Generally, if the creditworthiness of a bond weakens after you buy it, the bond's price will drop and its yield will rise to reflect the greater risk. Conversely, if the bond's credit quality improves, its value will increase and its yield will decline.

That's why you see a difference in the interest rate that two different issuers offer with the same maturity. For example, a five-year corporate bond would need to offer a higher rate of interest to attract your money than would a five-year government note. There is less perceived risk in loaning your money to the government than to a corporation whose recent earnings were reported lower than expected.

When you are trying to decide on which type of bonds to buy, not only must you be prepared to hold the bond until maturity, but you must also consider the amount of quality risk you are willing to assume. If you won't consider anything but "guaranteed" bonds, you must also be willing to accept lower rates of return than your peers who are willing to assume a little quality risk to earn a higher rate of return.

Risks Associated with Bonds

Like any other investment there are risks associated with bonds. There are two basic risks involved with bonds: *default risk* and *interest rate risk.*

You should be aware of both of these risks before you invest.

The most obvious way you can lose your money is when the issuer *defaults* on the bonds. In other words, the issuer doesn't have the ability to pay back your principal for the bonds. A classic example of this is the default of over 2 billion dollars worth of bonds issued by Washington Public Power System — known as WHOOPS. It doesn't happen very often but it can.

Before you buy any bond, you should check the credit quality of the issuer. You can do this by consulting a number of rating agencies like Moody's and Standard & Poor's. These rating agencies assign a credit rating based on the financial condition of the issuer offering the bonds. Unless you're speculating, most investors should stay with bonds that have a quality rating of AAA or AA.

Adventurous buyers might consider lower-quality issues. A bond rated BBB (lowest investment grade) offers a yield 1% to 2% higher than one rated AAA (highest rating). Bonds which are rated BB+ or lower are considered junk bonds and they offer even higher yields but carry with them considerably more risk.

The other way to lose money in bonds is *interest rate risk.* Let's go back to the mid 1970s when long-term government bonds were being offered at 8%. About five years later or by the early 1980s, inflation was running rampant at a rate of 12–13% and the government was forced to offer their long-term bonds at a rate much higher than normal. By 1980, you could buy that same bond at par and earn 14%! If you needed to sell that 8% bond, no one would give you par for the bond paying 8% because now they could pay par for a bond that was paying 14%. If you were forced to sell, you would only have been offered about $700 for each bond. That's a loss of $300 from your original investment of $1,000 per bond.

That is what happens to all bonds when interest rates rise. The longer the term of the bond, the more fluctuation it will be subject to. It has nothing to do with quality or its interest paying ability. It's simply that as interest rates rise, there are comparable bonds available with higher returns. Remember, *when interest rates rise, bond prices fall.*

This rule holds true with all bonds including corporate, government, municipal bonds and even bonds in mutual funds and unit investment trusts. You must be even more careful when buying bonds when interest rates are low. The lower the interest rate, the higher the probability that interest rates will be moving higher in the intermediate future which will force down the value of your bonds.

Interest rates, at any time, are impossible to predict with any great accuracy. If you wish to invest in bonds, the wisest course is to spread your money over a range of maturities, from as short as one or two years to no longer than 10 or 15 years.

By staggering maturities over time in this fashion, you will soon have money coming available that can be reinvested if interest rates go up. And if rates fall instead, you will have the satisfaction of owning a large number of bonds that are earning considerably more than the market is currently offering.

Some companies may choose to pay off all the bonds they've issued before the stated maturity in case interest rates drop sharply. This is called a *call provision.* This call provision allows the issuer to reissue new bonds at the new lower interest rate.

A call feature is part of the bond agreement which describes the schedule and price that the bonds may be given back to you. Typically, when bonds are called, they are redeemed at a premium price. A large number of bonds have been getting called in the late 1980s and early 1990s because of the high interest bonds issued during the early 1980s. Before considering a bond, be sure to ask if the bond is callable and at what price and date it could be called away.

Kinds of Bonds

Bond buyers have an abundance of choices when it comes to alternatives in the bond market. You must first, and most importantly, decide how much *quality* risk you are willing to assume. After deciding that, you will then have a lesser, but not small, number of alternatives available that could meet your objectives. You must then look over these alternatives with your financial consultant to best determine which bond best fits your needs.

The U.S. government issues bonds as well as do cities,

states, and corporations. These bonds can be bought through stock brokerage firms. Your decision on which bond is most appropriate for you depends on your individual needs. Not everyone's needs are the same. For example, a municipal bond would be a more appropriate choice for an individual in a high tax bracket than would that same bond for someone in the lowest tax bracket. Let's look at some of our alternatives.

Corporate Bonds

Corporate bonds are IOUs by a corporation. You are loaning your money to a corporation in exchange for interest. These companies may use the money to finance current operations, build new plants and equipment, and so on. The interest paid to the bondholders comes from the company's current earnings.

Corporate bonds are usually sold in minimum amounts of $1,000. The yield is subject to the current level of interest rates, the maturity, and the credit quality of the issuer. Because no corporation is considered to be as creditworthy or safe as the U.S. government, corporate bonds generally pay 1% to 2% more than comparable government bonds. Bond maturities range from 6 months to as many as 30 years. They pay interest semi-annually and the interest is subject to federal and state income taxes.

You may sell your bonds prior to maturity without a penalty and you will earn interest up to the day you sell your bond but you may get more or less than you originally paid depending on prevailing interest rates.

Commercial Paper

Not all corporate paper is necessarily long-term. One way a company can borrow money is by offering *commercial paper*. This type of debt has a stated maturity of not more than 270 days. Companies will offer this kind of paper when they need to borrow money for a short period of time.

Commercial paper can be bought through brokerage firms with minimum denominations of $25,000. Because the terms of the paper have such a short maturity, the yield is typically pretty low relative to longer-term bonds. Commercial paper is a popular choice for money market mutual fund accounts because of their short maturity.

Tax-Exempt Municipal Bonds

If you are in a relatively high income tax bracket, earning tax-free income can be an integral part of your savings strategy. Municipal bonds (popularly called *munis*) are one of the few remaining sources of tax-free income. These bonds are issued by cities, states, and other local bodies and political subdivisions. The bond issuers borrow the money they need by selling bonds, which are in effect IOUs.

The interest on the municipal bonds is unique. It is not subject to federal income taxes and may also be exempt from state and local taxes if you buy municipal bonds which are issued from your own state. This exemption is not the only reason to buy munis. They also yield high interest. Often they pay about 80% to 85% as much as U.S. Treasury bonds, but your interest from Treasuries is not exempt from federal taxes.

This income tax exemption reflects the longstanding American tradition that it's much to the public good to finance certain local projects, and so the nation can afford to give special tax incentives in these projects. State legislatures' and local governments' right to issue these tax-free bonds also essentially lowers their net interest costs.

There is no set difference in rates paid by munis and taxable bonds. Their rate is determined by the current level of interest rates, the credit rating of the issuer, and tax laws.

Interest is usually paid semiannually by the issuer. Maturities range from as short as a few months, known as municipal notes, to as long as 30 years. They may be sold prior to maturity at a premium or discount based on current interest rates. Next to U.S. government bonds, municipal bonds have been one of the safest of all such securities, with few exceptions.

There are two basic types of municipal bonds: *general obligation* and *revenue* bonds. Their classification comes from their payment source and according to their tax status. This is an important distinction.

General obligation (GO) bonds pay their interest from the revenues of the cities or states. The payments of principal and interest on GO bonds are secured by the full faith and credit of the state or local government that has *taxing* power. GO bonds are typically secured by their unlimited taxing power. That gives them a higher priority and level of safety than revenue bonds.

Revenue bonds are payable from a specific source of money usually the charges, tolls or rents from the facility being built. Highways, bridges, airports, hospitals, and water and sewer treatment plants are typical examples. Because the backing power of the bonds doesn't come from taxes but rather from the *revenues* of the project, these type of municipal bonds may be considered more risky than GO bonds and may offer higher yields.

Municipal notes are simply short-term issues with maturities of less than a year. They include tax-anticipation notes (TANs), bond anticipation notes (BANs), revenue anticipation notes (RANs), and tax and revenue anticipation notes (TRANs). Notes are usually issued to provide temporary funds and are repaid when anticipated revenues or taxes are collected, or when proceeds are received from a long-term bond issue.

In evaluating whether or not you should invest in municipal bonds, you will find it helpful to consider what another investment with a taxable yield would have to yield to be equivalent to the tax-free yield on the municipal bond.

To find the *taxable equivalent yield* on a tax-exempt investment, simply subtract your current tax bracket from 100 to get the remainder. Then divide the tax-free yield by the remainder. The result tells you how much you would have to earn from a taxable investment to equal the tax-free yield being offered.

For example, an investor in the 31% tax bracket would divide the municipal bond yield by 0.69. Here's an example. Let's say you were considering a municipal bond paying 6% and a taxable corporate bond paying 6%, both having similar maturities and credit quality ratings. Which of the two might make more sense for you, given you are in the 31% tax bracket?

You'd subtract your tax bracket (31) from 100, and get a remainder of 69. You'd then divide the 6% municipal yield by the remainder (0.69) and discover that you would have a tax equivalent yield of 8.7%. In other words, you would need to earn an 8.7% taxable yield to equal the 6% tax-free yield. So your choice would be obvious: Your after-tax return would be higher by selecting the 6% tax-free bond than the 6% taxable corporate bond.

Let's take a look at how taxes affect your investment's real returns. Again, let's assume an investor is in a 31% federal tax bracket and compare returns on two different 6% investments; one, a federal and state tax-free municipal bond and two, a taxable income investment like a CD. Notice the substantial affect taxes have on your after tax return.

Certificate of Deposit		Tax-Free Bond	
$100,000	Principal	$100,000	Principal
6.00%	Interest Rate	6.00%	Interest Rate
$6,000	Income Earned	$6,000	Income Earned
$6,000	Income Earned	$6,000	Income Earned
31%	Income Tax Rate	0%	Income Tax Rate
$1,860	Income Taxes Paid	$0	Income Taxes Paid
$6,000	Income Earned	$6,000	Income Earned
$1,860	Income Taxes Paid	$0	Income Taxes Paid
$4,140	After-Tax Income	$6,000	After-Tax Income

Some investors simply buy municipal bonds with the intention of avoiding paying taxes to the government. This may not always be the wisest decision. The higher your tax bracket, the bigger the tax advantages become. If you are in a lower tax bracket, your taxable equivalent spread becomes much less advantageous.

Before you buy tax-free bonds, figure out how the yield compares with the after-tax return you could get on alternative investments. It is not how much taxes you don't pay, but how much you have left after taxes over a period of time that will determine which was the best investment.

Some municipal securities' principal and interest are insured against default by private insurers such as the Municipal Bond Insurance Association (MBIA) and the American Municipal Bond Assurance Corporation (AMBAC). The insured municipal bonds' yields are generally lower than non-insured bonds because the costs of the insurance are passed on to the bondholder.

As with any other investment, if you buy only the highest quality municipals, the chances of default are very, very low. If, however, the insurance will help you rest at night, then perhaps insured bonds might be worth considering.

Junk Bonds

High-yield bonds is the term that this group of bonds prefers to call itself. (*Junk bonds* sounds a little too incriminating.) High-yield bonds are IOUs issued by a corporation with very high rates of interest. The reason they pay such a high yield is that there is a strong possibility that the issuing company may not be able to earn enough money to pay its interest payments. Junk bonds earn a low grade from rating services such as Standard & Poor's or Moody's. They either have no rating at all or are rated BB+ or lower by S&P and BA1 or lower by Moody's.

High-yield bonds carry the same risks as any other type of bonds. The biggest risk, however, is risk of default. The late 1980s and early 1990s saw record numbers of defaults in junk bonds. Many of the bonds were involved in the Drexel Burnham scandal.

There are good high-yield bonds and there are bad ones. It is important to check the ratings, do your homework, and decide whether the high yield is worth the inherent default risk. You must carefully consider the risk-reward trade-off.

Convertible Bonds

Convertible bonds, some would say, are the best of both worlds. You are buying a bond, but also buying the right, at a specific time down the road, to convert your bond into common stock of the issuing company.

The convertible bond pays a fixed interest rate for a fixed period of time. But the bond buyer has the right to convert the bond into a certain number of shares at a certain price. If the company does well and its stock price rises, the bondholder can convert the bond into the stock and participate in the stock's profits. If the company doesn't do so great and the stock goes nowhere, you will still have the security of collecting regular interest payments from the convertible bond.

Federal Agency Securities

In addition to Treasuries, the safest of all government bonds, there is another group of securities that falls under the umbrella of government bonds. These are considered agency securities. Most are issued by associations or agencies created by Congress, and many are either backed or guaranteed by the government. They are only slightly inferior to the Treasuries; to compensate, they carry a slightly higher yield. The most popular of these securities is Ginnie Mae.

Ginnie Maes

Ginnie Mae (GNMA) is a security issued by the Government National Mortgage Association and backed by the mortgages that the wholly owned U.S. government corporation holds. When you invest in a GNMA, you are buying a share in a pool of fixed-rate home mortgages insured by the Federal Housing Administration. Ginnie Maes give investors a high degree of security because of this federal backing.

Ginnie Maes pay regular interest on a monthly basis over a period of years. The interest rates on these bonds are usually just slightly higher than the rates on long-term government bonds. But there's a reason they pay a slightly higher rate. You don't know exactly when you will get all your principal paid back to you.

Because you own a pool of home mortgages, you will get principal returned to you when homeowners pay off their mortgages. These types of bonds have what is called an *average life*. Average life simply means that the bond's maturity is not known for certain. Its maturity is affected by the direction of interest rates.

Falling interest rates induce people to refinance their mortgages. When those mortgages are repaid, you get your principal and interest back, and your Ginnie Mae investment unit is liquidated sooner than you may have expected. If, on the other hand, interest rates rise, homeowners may decide to hold on to their mortgages longer than expected; the actual maturity of your GNMA will lengthen.

That is why these types of mortgage-backed bonds have *average lives.* You can never be certain how much money you will receive each month and how long these installments will last. Homeowners' payment schedules change with economic conditions, and so change the maturity on your mortgage-backed bonds. The risk of not knowing exactly when you'll get back all of your money is why these bonds pay a slightly higher rate of interest than do regular government bonds.

GNMA bonds typically pay a monthly income and can be bought with an average life of a few months to 30 years. Most often their average life is 10 to 12 years. Their minimum normally is $25,000, but brokerage firms and mutual fund companies will allow you to buy these securities for as little as $1,000.

One last cautionary note: Like any other type of bond, if interest rates rise, the value of GNMAs will fall. But when interest rates fall the value of GNMAs won't shoot up in price, at least not to a very large premium like most bonds.

Why? Because when interest rates fall, homeowners refinance their mortgages and principal is paid off. Buyers are not willing to pay a very large premium for bonds that may be called away at any time at par.

Zero Coupon Bonds

Zero coupon bonds became very popular in the 1980s. They are a type of bond that is issued at a deep discount from face value. With a zero you pay, for example, $500 today for something that will be worth $1,000 at maturity. The bonds are issued at a discount much like the Series EE savings bonds. The big difference is that you pay taxes on the accumulated interest as it is earned each year, even though you don't actually receive any interest from the zero which is maturing in the future. The IRS wants you to report the interest that you will eventually receive. The one exception to this rule is municipal zeros. They free the purchaser of the worry about paying taxes on the imputed interest, since the interest may be tax exempt.

Zero coupon bonds are one of the most volatile types of bonds available. You must be prepared for big price swings in value. If interest rates move up and you need to sell your bonds before maturity, you may sustain a major loss. On the other hand, if interest rates drop after you buy the zero, you could have a substantial gain in a very short time.

The potential for large principal fluctuation is why zero coupon bonds became so popular in the 1980s. As interest rates fell during the decade, speculators bought the appreciating bonds with the intention of selling them as interest rates declined. Investors had nearly a decade of falling interest rates with bond prices rising rapidly.

Zeros can be an excellent way to save for the future because you know ahead of time exactly what you'll be getting. They are most often used for planning ahead for children's college education expenses.

Zero coupon investments have been structured from corporate and municipal bonds, CDs, and U.S. Treasuries. No matter which zero investment you choose, it will always be priced at a substantial discount from its face value. The longer the maturity, the greater the discount.

Chapter 4: Stocks

The stock market has been a real hero for a large number of investors and a real sore spot for others. You will hear countless stories of people who made a killing in the market and others who lost their shirts. While some of these tales may be true, the simple fact is that if you are a long-term investor, the probability of your money outperforming inflation with stocks is much greater than with any other type of investment. That's the goal of most investors — to create a higher standard of living (outpace inflation) for the future. Stocks are the only investment that has consistently outpaced inflation.

Understanding Stocks

A share of stock represents ownership in a corporation. A corporation is owned by its stockholders — often thousands of people and institutions, each owning a fraction of the corporation.

When you buy a stock in a corporation you become a part-owner or stockholder. You immediately own a part, no matter how small, of every building, piece of office furniture, machinery, or whatever that company owns.

As a shareholder, you stand to profit when the company profits. You are also legally entitled to a say in major policy decisions, such as whether to issue additional stock, sell the company to outside buyers, or change the board of directors. The general rule is that each share has the same voting power, so the more shares you own, the greater your power. You can vote in person by attending a corporation's annual meeting. Or you can vote by using an absentee ballot, called a *proxy*, which is mailed before each meeting.

A stock does not have a fixed, objective worth. At any moment, it's only as valuable as people think. When you buy a stock, you're making a bet that a lot of other people are going to want to buy that stock too — and, as a result, the price will go up.

The stock market is, however, more than a lot of investors watching what other investors do. Investors and analysts also watch the companies and their future prospects very carefully. Since the value of shares is directly related to how well the company is doing, investors naturally look for the companies with the best prospects for strong, sustained earnings.

How do you judge a company's prospects? By current or anticipated earnings, the desirability of its product or service, the competition, availability of new markets, management strengths and many other considerations. These are the factors that stock analysts watch in trying to predict whether a stock's value will rise or fall.

How do you make money in stocks? As a rule, the better a company does and the higher its profits, the more money its stockholders make. Investors buy stocks to make money in one or both of two ways:

- Through dividend payments while you own the stock, or
- By selling the stock for more than you paid.

Most companies parcel out portions of their annual profits to stockholders in the form of quarterly *dividend* payments. Dividend payments vary from stock to stock. Stocks with consistent histories of paying high dividends are known as *income stocks.* Investors often buy income stocks for their current dividends rather than for the company's future growth prospects.

Some companies, however, reinvest most of their profits back into the business in order to expand and strengthen. As a result, companies that pay little or no dividend are called *growth stocks* because investors expect the company to grow — and the stock price to grow with it.

Why do companies issue stock? When stocks are traded in the market, the company doesn't make a cent on the deal. A company only makes money when the new stock is issued, or put up for sale. The first time a company's stock is issued, the company is said to be *going public.* In other words, the owners of the company are selling part ownership to the general public. The formal name for this process is an *initial public offering (IPO).*

Typically, a company offers stock when it needs to raise money, usually for expansion. In exchange for the cash, the company management gives up some of the decision-making control to the shareholders. When a company goes public, it also benefits from the fact that its stock is trading in the open market. This trading tends to give the company legitimacy: Its performance, its financial vitality, becomes visible to all.

The stock market goes through cycles, trending upward for periods of time, then reversing itself, and vice versa. A rising period is known as a *bull market* — bulls being the market optimists who cause prices to rise. A *bear market* is a falling market, where the pessimists are driving prices lower. The stock market is a constant struggle between the bulls and the bears, both groups tugging in opposite directions.

Sometimes market trends last a long time, even years. Overall, though, bull markets usually continue for longer periods of time than bear markets.

Common Stock

Common stock owners typically are entitled to vote on the selection of directors and other important matters as well as to receive dividends on their holdings. In the event that a corporation is liquidated, the claims of secured and un-secured creditors and owners of bonds and preferred stock take precedence over the claims of those who own common stock. For the most part, common stock has more potential for appreciation.

Preferred Stock

Preferred stock pays dividends at a specified rate and has preference over common stock in the payment of dividends and the liquidation of assets. The dividend is usually higher than the common stock dividend.

The term "preferred" does not mean "better." It relates only to dividend precedence. Preferred stock does not ordinarily carry voting rights. If the preferred stock is also convertible to common stock, it will have a conversion ratio into the common and take some of the characteristics of the company's common stock.

Types of Stocks by Performance

If you wanted to maximize your growth potential you might want to take a look at *growth* stocks. Growth stocks are stocks that show a better-than-average appreciation over a period of time. Their sales, earnings and market share are expanding faster than the general economy and the industry average. The key to success is picking these stocks in advance of their strongest period of growth. Because of the uncertainty, growth stocks are called *speculative* and their price may fluctuate a great deal. These stocks are characterized by low dividend yields and high price/earnings (PE) ratios.

To be successful at selecting growth stocks, you must be aware of current events: Consumer psychology plays a big part in the valuation of growth stocks. You must also keep track of which industries are presently most dominant. These industries are where the most growth will come from, and thus, where the stock market's biggest winners will emerge.

You need to look for companies with consistent annual increasing growth in earnings and sales, even in the face of poor economic conditions. These companies normally have a new product or service that people need or want.

Some people only prefer to stick with the big-name companies with proven sales and track records. *Blue chip* stocks make a good choice for those who want to invest their money in a well known company. Blue chip is a term used to describe a well-established company that has demonstrated its ability to pay dividends in good and bad times.

The term *blue chip* was introduced in 1904 to describe the stocks of the largest, most consistently profitable corporations. The term comes from the blue chips used in poker — always the most valuable chips. They are simply common stocks of nationally known companies that have a long record of profit growth and dividend payments and a reputation for high-quality management and services.

If you're looking for the next stock to double within three months or so, a *special situation stock* might give you the best chance. A special situation stock is stock in a company whose potential is not reflected in its day-to-day operations. A new management team, a technological breakthrough or similar occurrence can cause speculation for new growth in the future.

Some stocks do relatively well regardless of the economic times. *Defensive stocks* are not subject to the variations of the business cycle. They have a resistance to a recession. Examples are food chains, utilities and tobacco companies. People will use gas and electricity and smoke during bad economic periods as well as during good times.

If you are looking for a stock that pays a higher rate of return, you might consider an *income* stock. Its dividends are high relative to the market price. This type of stock is generally attractive to those who buy stocks for income.

If you are dependent on income for your groceries and if the price of groceries continues to rise, you must increase your income to keep pace with the rise in food prices. Many income stocks have raised their dividends (income) year after year for many, many years. This type of stock investment makes a lot of sense for people who need a rising income stream to keep pace with inflation. Most public utilities are considered income stocks.

It is important that you don't reach too far for high yields in income stocks, however. Normally, the reason a stock's yield is abnormally high is that the company is paying out an inordinately large percentage of its earnings, which could adversely affect future earnings. Another reason a stock may have an unusually high yield is that the market has given the company a poor evaluation for future prospects. Thus, you may be risking your capital; the stock's price may fall considerably. In other words, if it looks to good to be true, it probably is!

In selecting stocks for dependable income, you'll want to choose quality issues with long, established dividend records rather than younger, less tested companies who haven't been in business long enough to establish an extended dividend paying record.

Some stocks coming out of a recession do better than others. *Cyclical* stocks are stocks of companies whose earnings fluctuate with the general business cycle. If you were looking to maximize your stock returns and wanted to take advantage of the rise in the economy's profitability, these cyclical stocks might be a good choice.

When business conditions improve, the company's profitability is restored and the common stock price rises. When economic conditions deteriorate, the company's business falls off and its profits are diminished. This causes the cyclical stock's price to decline. Steel, cement, machine tools and automobiles are some of the groups of stocks you might look for to find investments that fit into your portfolio.

Finally, can you believe that stocks can change with the weather? Some stocks have seasonal changes; they are called *seasonal* stocks. These are stocks of companies whose earnings have a tendency to fluctuate with the year's seasons. Retail companies represent a good example. Their sales and profits will generally increase at certain times of the year, such as Christmas and the opening of school.

Stock Characteristics

If you take the number of shares of stock outstanding of a company and multiply that number by the stock's current price, you will find the total market value of that company. If a company has 500 million shares outstanding and each share is worth $20, then the market value of that company is $10 billion. This is one way to compare the size of two companies.

To compare how well a company is doing, look at its *sales*. If a company's sales are increasing, there is a good possibility that the company is earning money. Analysts look at the sales that are reported on a quarterly basis and compare them to last year's sales figures. If the sales increases meet or exceed expectations, the stock's price should go up. This figure is just one of many used to determine the value of a company.

Another is to look at a company's *earnings*. Publicly traded companies calculate and report their earnings quarterly (every three months). Analysts and stock buyers watch for the earnings figure to see how well it compares with last year's quarterly earnings. If the earnings reported are better than last year's or better than expected, the company's stock price rises. If the company reports poor earnings for the quarter, its stock price normally drops.

Stock analysts take the earnings reported and divide that number by the number of shares outstanding to get a number called the *earnings per share*. This figure represents how much money the company is making per share of stock outstanding.

Another figure stock buyers and analysts look at is the stock's *price/earnings ratio* (PE ratio). The PE ratio is the price of a share of stock divided by earnings per share for a 12-month period. In other words, it's the price of a stock relative to its earnings. If a stock has a price of $50 and is earning $2.50 a share, it is said to be selling at a PE ratio of 20 to 1. In other words, its selling price is 20 times last year's earnings.

A general rule to follow is that the Dow's PE averages around 15 historically. It can fluctuate greatly, and it does in extreme times. Smaller growth companies have higher future growth and earnings expectations; it follows that this type of company has a higher PE ratio. The more mature, slower-growing companies tend to have a lower PE ratio.

One cautionary note: *A low* PE ratio doesn't necessarily mean that a company is undervalued and a high PE ratio doesn't necessarily mean that the company is overpriced. There are reasons why stocks have high prices and low prices; these don't include that it's simply a great buy or a time to sell. Stocks usually sell for what they're worth at that time.

Out of a company's earnings come *dividends*. Dividends are to stocks what interest is to bonds/CDs. A dividend is the term used by stocks to describe a payment to shareholders. Most people are familiar with dividends paid by utility companies. But a large number of other companies also pay a dividend.

Smaller growth companies don't normally pay dividends. They like to keep their earnings to reinvest back into the company for expansion. Reinvesting their earnings helps them avoid going to the bank or to the market to borrow for their future growth.

Dividends are paid out of a company's earnings. For example, let's say a company paid a total annual $2 dividend per share. If you owned 100 shares of that company, you would get a dividend payment of $200 for the year. Dividends are paid on a quarterly basis. In the previous case, every three months you'd receive a dividend check for $50 ($50 x 4 = $200).

If you had invested $5,000 in a stock and it pays you a dividend of $200, you would be receiving a 4% dividend return. Of course, the value of the stock can move up or down; that changes your total return.

Companies declare their dividends ahead of time. The interval between the announcement of the dividend and the actual payment date is called the ex-dividend date. An investor who buys shares during that interval is not entitled to the dividend. You must be owner of record before the ex-dividend date. The ex-dividend date is the date on which a stock goes ex-dividend, typically about one to three weeks before the dividend is paid to shareholders of record. Typically, a stock's price moves up by the dollar amount of the dividend as the ex-dividend date approaches, then falls by the amount of the dividend after that date.

When stocks rise in price rapidly, some companies choose to split their stock. A *stock split* is a way to reduce a stock's price to a more marketable level for the average investor. More investors will consider buying a stock that is priced at $30 per share than one priced at $100. One hundred shares at $30 is only $3,000, but 100 shares of the second total $10,000.

If a company decides to split its stock priced at $60 per share at 2 for 1, the 100 shares you presently own ($6,000 worth) are increased to 200 shares. But the value of each share is simultaneously split in half; your net value doesn't change. After the split you have 200 shares priced at $30 per share; your net value remains at $6,000.

Reverse splits also happen, but not as often. In this case the value of the stock is increased while the number of shares you own is decreased.

Where Do You Buy Stocks?

You need to buy stocks through a broker. The business of a broker is to find the best price available and to provide timely, sound investment advice that meets your individual financial goals. Only a broker can execute an order to buy or sell stocks. They spend, or should spend, a lot of time researching investments, helping clients develop goals, and giving advice. *Discount brokers* act strictly as agents for your transactions and do not offer investment advice.

Each time you buy or sell stock, you pay a *commission.* A portion of that commission goes to your broker. The rest goes to the firm to cover costs associated with the transaction.

Stocks are traded either on an *exchange* (listed) or *over the counter* (unlisted). *Listed* means that the stock is listed and traded on a national or regional exchange. These exchanges are an organized marketplace in which stocks and bonds are traded by members of the exchange. They have a physical location where brokers and dealers meet to execute orders from institutional and individual investors to buy and sell securities. Our four largest exchanges are the New York Stock Exchange, the American Stock Exchange, the Pacific Stock Exchange and the Midwest Stock Exchange. Each exchange sets its own requirements for membership.

The shares of most large companies in the U.S. are publicly traded on the *New York Stock Exchange* (NYSE) or the *American Stock Exchange.* There are over 2,000 stocks listed on the NYSE and over 1,000 stocks listed on the American Stock Exchange. The number of stocks listed on the exchanges is constantly changing because new companies are listed and others can be delisted. Stocks may be delisted for no longer meeting the exchange's financial standards.

There are also a number of smaller regional exchanges such as the Pacific Stock Exchange, the Philadelphia Stock Exchange, the Boston Stock Exchange and the Cincinnati Stock Exchange. These regional exchanges typically make a market for regional, smaller, local companies.

The New York Stock Exchange

The New York Stock Exchange is the oldest and largest. To my knowledge, extended documentation of its history has yet to be written. Some say it started as early as 1725, when the market dealt in commodities such as wheat and tobacco. Others say it began very informally near the time of the birth of our nation when our first Secretary of the Treasury needed to set up a monetary system. One thing seems certain: In both cases, investors are said to have met under a tree at the foot of a street in New York called "Wall." They eventually moved indoors; from this beginning emerged the New York Stock Exchange.

The New York Stock Exchange (NYSE) accounts for 90% of the business transacted on all organized exchanges in the U.S. The NYSE has the most stringent requirements for companies to meet to be listed on its exchange.

Let's say you decided to buy 100 shares of Wal-Mart. Your order to buy Wal-Mart stock would be sent via computer to a location on the floor of the NYSE. There, a *specialist* who deals with Wal-Mart stock would receive your order and would then try to match your buy order with a sell order from someone else at a price similar to the previous trade's price.

A specialist is one whose job is to maintain a fair and orderly market in specific securities, like Wal-Mart stock. If the specialists cannot match the buy and sell orders, they are obligated to use their own capital to buy or sell shares in that stock. If there is an overabundance of buy orders to buy Wal-Mart, the specialist will sell some stock out of his or her own inventory at higher and higher prices. If there is an overabundance of sell orders coming in, the specialist will buy the shares for his or her own inventory at lower and lower prices. Specialists' role is simply to maintain an orderly market.

The Over-the-Counter Market

If you're looking for stocks that are more risky but may offer you substantial rewards, you might want to shop in the *over-the-counter* (OTC) market. The OTC market tends to be made up of companies that are too small and too new to be listed on the major exchanges.

The main purpose of the OTC market is to provide a market for new issues and secondary issues of unlisted securities, and to facilitate trading in unlisted securities already issued and publicly held. Many great growth issues have emerged from the OTC market over the years: McDonald's and Wendy's are only two of the familiar names that started there.

However, the OTC market involves much more than just stocks. It is the market for all transactions which do *not* take place on an exchange. With minor exceptions, this includes all trading in U.S. government and agency securities, money market instruments, municipal bonds, and mutual funds. Corporate bonds also trade quite frequently in this market. The OTC *stock* market is best known to investors, however.

The OTC market does not have a physical trading floor where stocks are traded like the exchanges. Instead, it is an electronic marketplace linked by computers. Market makers or dealers working for brokerage firms keep an inventory of the stock and set buy and sell (bid and offer) prices. These prices are shown on computer screens at dealer firms around the country. This computer system is called NASDAQ — the National Association of Securities Dealers Automated Quote system. It provides quotations from dealers willing to buy and sell shares on a continuous basis for their own account or for accounts for brokers who phone in with orders.

The NASDAQ listings have an abundant number of small, unnoticed companies, some of which are selling at very low prices. They may be undervalued because too few people have taken a look at their financial statements.

This is not a market for the faint-hearted. Though you may find tomorrow's big winner here, you may also find the future's big loser. The OTC market is typically where the hot stock tips come from. *Beware!* The big winners in this market are those small companies that are major competitors in emergent fields.

Penny stocks are stocks that typically sell for less that $5 a share. They may just be low-priced stocks, high-risk stocks, or potential rip offs! Many times they rise rapidly right after they start trading, usually because of heavy promotion, possibly because they have been manipulated by unscrupulous securities firms.

The Securities and Exchange Commission (SEC) has created a rule that requires that a broker must determine, in writing, that penny stocks are suitable investments for you. The broker must get financial information and the customer's investment experience before any trade is binding.

On the other side of the coin is the possibility for huge gains. Some companies may be down in the doldrums because of horrid earnings, or may be emerging from bankruptcy and have a bright future ahead of them because of a new product or promising breakthrough. Some of these stocks trade on the New York Stock Exchange. A majority are listed in the *pink sheets*.

The pink sheets are a listing of bid and offer prices of low priced stocks by dealers, along with their phone numbers. Pink sheet stocks are stocks that are traded too infrequently to be listed on the NASDAQ system. These types of stocks should generally be avoided by most investors because of their thinly traded markets. These companies are generally very small and it is difficult to get a lot of information about them.

The important thing to remember is that you are taking a lot more risk than you would normally take buying mature blue chip stocks. Finally, look for three warning signs of penny-stock fraud: unsolicited phone calls, high pressure sales tactics, and the inability to sell the stock and receive cash.

Market Indices

"How did the market do today?"

That question is usually answered with a reference to the *Dow Jones Industrial Average (DJIA)*, comprised of 30 stocks listed on the New York Stock Exchange. The Dow is the most widely followed stock market average. The Dow Jones Average is actually made up of four averages — the Industrial, the Composite, the Utility and the Transportation. The best known is the Industrial.

The DJIA was developed by Charles Dow back in 1884. Then it was comprised of only 11 stocks. In 1916 the Dow added nine stocks to its average. The average was broadened in 1928 to include its present number of 30 stocks. The Dow's 30 stocks are blue-chip companies that represent about 25% of the market value of stocks listed on the New York Stock Exchange.

The DJIA is considered a barometer of the stock market and the economy. The 30 stocks in the Dow are the companies that best represent our economy. Back in the early 1900s the Dow was made up mostly of industrial companies like steel and railroads. Those companies best represented our economy back then. Today our economy is made up of more service-type corporations; the DJIA reflects that with companies like McDonald's that are part of the average.

Calculating the Dow Jones Industrial Average is not as simple as adding all 30 stock prices and dividing by 30. The DJIA average is price-weighted — that is, the total of component stock prices is divided by a divisor. As a result, a high-priced stock has a greater influence on the index than a low-priced stock. This means that one or two stocks can distort the average with significant price fluctuations.

For example, let's say that 29 of the 30 Dow stocks ended

Dow Jones Industrial Average

Allied-Signal Inc.	ALD	Int'l Business Machines	IBM
Aluminum Co. of America	AA	International Paper	IP
American Express	AXP	J.P. Morgan & Co.	JPM
American Tel. & Tel.	T	McDonald's Corp.	MCD
Bethlehem Steel	BS	Merck & Co.	MRK
Boeing Co.	BA	Minn Mining & Mfg.	MMM
Caterpillar Inc.	CAT	Philip Morris	MO
Chevron Corp.	CHV	Proctor & Gamble	PG
Coca–Cola Co.	KO	Sears Roebuck	S
DuPont (E.I.)	DD	Texaco Inc.	TX
Eastman Kodak	EK	Union Carbide	UK
Exxon Corp.	XON	United Technologies	UTX
General Electric	GE	Walt Disney Co.	DIS
General Motors	GM	Westinghouse Electric	WX
Goodyear Tire	GT	Woolworth Corp.	Z

the day's trading with just slight increases, while one high-priced stock included in the Dow went down $10 per share. What would that do to the average? It would probably show a down close; people would then assume the market was down. But the overall market was not necessarily down, even though the Dow reflected a down day.

What might give us a better indicator of how the market did today? The *Standard & Poor's 500* (S&P 500) stock index may give us a better reading of the "barometer" of the market. The index is made up of 400 industrial, 20 transportation, 40 utility, and 40 financial stocks.

The S&P 500 is a list of stocks that are traded on the NYSE, the American Stock Exchange and the OTC market. However, the index consists primarily of NYSE-listed stocks. Not only is this a broader list of stocks than the DJIA; it is a market-weighted index. That means each stock influences the index in proportion to the number of its shares outstanding and the market value of those shares. Because of this, the index cannot be influenced significantly by one or two stocks and is why many use this index as a barometer to measure the market.

There are many other averages that you can watch to follow the markets. The American Stock Exchange Market Value Index, OTC Index, the Wilshire 5000 Equity Index and the NYSE Composite Index are just a few others that investors like to watch. Investors and traders like to watch more specific indexes, such as the drug, utility, or bank stock indexes. The drug stock index measures the values of drug companies. The utility and bank stock indexes measure the value of utility and bank stocks.

How Stocks Are Analyzed

Before you buy a stock, the first thing you must do is to decide which one to buy. No problem, right? Well, it all depends on how you go about it. On paper, figuring out which stock to buy can make factual sense ... but facts alone won't guarantee success. The other part of the stock selection process involves consumer psychology and unexpected events.

Unfortunately, we cannot quantify investor psychology or predict the unexpected easily. Some stocks on paper may not look too healthy but, because of investor expectations, the stock may rise for many years. Obviously it's pretty hard to predict unexpected events. Stocks react — most often negatively — to unexpected events, especially world unrest. Because we cannot control psychology or predict future events, we need to use other ways to evaluate stocks.

There are two major schools of thought on picking stocks. Many serious investors swear by *fundamental analysis*. Fundamental analysis involves appraising a company's financial condition and management, as well as its competitive position in its industry.

Other investors live and die by *technical analysis*. Technical analysis ignores fundamentals, instead using charts of past performance to identify price trends and cyclical movements of particular stocks, industries or the market as a whole.

Those who feel every factor must be considered synthesize the two and form an opinion using both methods. Finally, there is the less time consuming method of throwing darts at the stock page. I wouldn't recommend this last strategy, but to each his own.

Fundamental Analysis

Fundamental analysis involves an estimate of the stock's *value* by looking at the basic facts about the company. Once the company's value is determined, it is compared to the stock's current market price. If the stock's market price is lower than the value of the company, investment firms recommend purchasing the stock. If the company's value is lower than the current market price of the stock, then typically the investment firm will recommend that you sell the stock.

Critical to fundamental analysis is the evaluation of *earnings*, particularly future earnings. Fundamental analysts cite the expectation of future earnings as the most important variable affecting stock prices. If a company is not expected to make money in the next couple quarters or years, its stock price is going to have a tough time going up. Analysts also look at how well a company has done in the last 10 years for an idea of what is it capable of earning.

Book value is the company's real net worth. It is found by subtracting its liabilities from its assets. Analysts like to see if the company's stock is selling for more or less than the book value per share. If it is trading at less than its book value, it may be underpriced.

Fundamental analysts want to see how much *debt* a company has. A company's *balance sheet* gives a real picture of the company's assets (equity) and liabilities (debt). Watch out for unusually large amounts of long-term debt. A company should not have a high debt-to-equity ratio relative to the average for its industry.

Another factor fundamentalists look at is *management capability*. Is management responsive to changes in technology? Are they on the cutting edge? Do they invest in their people? Analysts will literally call on management and ask about their company and its future prospects.

Where can you get this information? You can find most of it in the company's *annual report*. This report is sent out once a year. It lists, in detailed form, how the company has performed in the last year. For the average investor, digesting this financial information and making sense of it are a pretty big bite to chew. Without a sound financial education, the numbers may not make a lot of sense.

You can simplify your understanding of a company's financial condition with information available from other sources. Both *Value Line* and *Standard & Poor's Stock Guide* will give you financial information in a more simplified form. They give descriptions of the company's business, its recent earnings, future earnings estimates, and the outlook for the company's industry. These reports are basically created for informational purposes.

Another place to find financial information is in *research reports* issued by brokerage firms. They are tailored in form so investors can easily read and digest the information. The brokerage firm analyst talks to management and makes a recommendation on the stock based on his or her projections or earnings estimates.

Fundamental analysts also look at the general economic

picture. They are concerned with the direction of interest rates and inflation. In general, they want to the know which direction the economy is headed. An understanding of where the economy is today and where it is headed tomorrow helps them determine whether a company's stock is over or under-priced relative to economic conditions.

Technical Analysis

Technical analysis involves looking at the past sequence of stock prices. Its concern is with the historical movement of the stock's price. Unlike the fundamentalists who look at companies' value based on earnings, the *technicians* focus on price patterns and volume figures. They use dozens of different techniques to interpret those figures. They say that stock prices generally tend to move in trends that persist for significant periods of time. They maintain that chart patterns often tend to recur. These recurring patterns can be used to forecast future prices.

Technicians love to use charts. They record past prices and other technical data like volume to see which way a trend is forming. If a technical trend is rising, they consider it a good sign for stocks. If trends are moving down, they consider it a negative and may recommend a sell on the investment. Let's look at a few of the more universal technical tools.

One tool technicians emphasize is *trading volume*. Trading volume is the number of shares changing hands. When a stock's price is moving up or down with a lot of volume, technicians say that the stock's movement is significant. If the stock is trading with less than normal volume, its price movement is less significant.

Some analysts construct *moving averages* of stock prices by adding together, for example, the last 200 days' closing prices of a stock and then comparing it to today's price. Calculating the moving average tends to eliminate the effect of short-term fluctuations.

The moving averages provide technicians with a couple key price levels: the *resistance level* and *support level*. For example, analysts consider a downward penetration through a moving-average line (support) as a signal to sell. On the other hand, if stocks rise above its resistance level, technicians might consider this a reason to buy the stock.

Another tool technicians use is the *advance/decline line*. The advance/decline line is simply the daily count of stocks that rise and the number that fall. When the gainers (more stocks rising than falling) outnumber the losers (more stocks falling than rising), analysts consider this a sign that the market is getting stronger. When losers predominate, analysts consider it a weakness in the market.

How To Buy Stocks

Once you've made the decision about which stock or stocks to buy, you must then decide on a method to purchase them. While there are a large number of sophisticated ways to buy stocks, we'll look at a few of the strategies that the average investor should understand.

If you've found tomorrow's winner, are ready to buy it, and are willing to pay the current market price, you will enter a market order. A *market order* requires you accept the current price of the stock when the order reaches the trading floor. Most orders executed on the exchanges are market orders. If you've decided to buy a stock, you normally enter a market order to buy the stock.

If you want to buy or sell a particular stock but aren't willing to buy or sell it at the current market price then you can enter a *limit order*. A limit order means that you have placed an order to buy or sell a stock at a specified price. The specialist won't fill (buy or sell the stock) the order until the stock reaches the price you specified in the limit order.

For example, let's say you want to buy Wal-Mart at a stock price of $30; it is currently trading at $33. You could put in a limit order to buy Wal-Mart at $30. This means that your order will not fill unless Wal-Mart stock traded down to at least $30.

On the other hand, if you put in a limit order to sell at $35, your stock will not sell until the price reaches or exceeds $35. If it never reaches $35, your sell order will never execute.

If you want an order to be in effect for only one day, you can use a *day order;* your order will only be in effect for one day. If you feel sure the stock's price is going to meet your price expectations, you can also enter an *open order,* or *good-'til-canceled* order. This type of order gives the specialist the permission to execute your open order at any later date if the price of the stock should return to your limit price.

One way to keep from losing all your money in a particular stock is by using a *stop order.* A stop order is an order to buy or sell at a specified price, called the stop price.

A stop order to buy, always at a stop price above the current market price, is usually designed to protect a profit or limit a loss on a short sell. A stop order to sell, always at a price below the current market price, is usually designed to protect a profit or to limit a loss on a security already purchased at a higher price. The risk of stop orders is that they may be triggered by temporary market movement or be executed at prices higher or lower than the stop price because of market orders ahead of them.

When you buy stocks you must decide how many shares to buy. As a general rule, you should try to buy stocks in *round lots.* Round lots consist of 100 shares or more. Purchases of fewer than 100 shares at a time are called *odd lots.*

If you buy less than a round lot (100 shares), you may pay a higher commission rate. The difference is usually about ⅛ of a point (12½ cents) per share. For example, someone buying 100 shares of XYZ at $50 may pay $50 a share plus commission. At the same time, another who buys only 50 shares of XYZ would pay 50⅛ per share plus commission.

If you don't have a lot to invest, don't buy 100 shares only to save ⅛ of a point. Either buy the odd lot to prevent becoming overweighted in one stock, or consider a mutual fund that will give you the benefits of diversification with smaller investments.

Selling Short

You've heard the old adage—"Buy low, sell high!"

Well, for those contrarians out there, there is a strategy used by some who "sell high, buy low!" It is called *selling short.*

Investors who believe that a stock is overpriced and expect it to decline in the future might choose to sell short. A short sale is the sale of a security that is not owned with the intention of repurchasing it later at a lower price. The investor borrows the security from another investor through a broker and sells it in the market. Later, the investor will repurchase the security and return it to the broker. The fee for borrowing the stock is the interest on the money that the stock represents. The short seller pays this interest fee.

Here's how it works. Let's say you sold short 100 shares of a stock at $50 a share. The proceeds of the sale ($5,000) will be credited to your margin account. The proceeds must stay in the account, plus you must put up 50% of the market value of the stock to ensure the there will be money available to rebuy at some point in the future.

If the stock drops from $50 to $35, you will rebuy the position (*cover* your shorts) by going into the market and purchasing 100 shares of the stock at a cost of $3,500. Your profit on the short sale is $1,500. The brokerage firm then restores the borrowed stock with the newly purchased stock.

If the stock you've shorted drops as expected, all is fine and dandy. But what happens if the stock rises after you've sold short? What if the stock you shorted at $50 goes to $70, then $80, or even up to $100? Because you borrowed the stock, at some point you have to return it. If the stock price rises, you will have to buy it to prevent more losses if it goes even higher.

The biggest risk with short selling is that you have the potential for unlimited losses. That is, there is unlimited potential for the stock to rise, and therefore unlimited potential for loss. On the other hand, you do have limited potential for gain. A stock sold short at $50 can only earn $50 per share.

There are two technical points relevant to short sales. First, a short sale can only be made on an *uptick*. In other words, you can only sell a stock short when the previous differently priced sale was slightly higher (⅛ of a point or more). This prevents traders from forcing a profit on a short sale by pushing the price down by continually selling short. Secondly, the short seller is responsible for the dividends to the investor who loaned the stock. The short seller receives the dividend from the corporation; because he or she doesn't really own it, the short seller must pay that dividend amount to the investor who loaned the stock.

Foreign Stocks

As the economy becomes increasingly global in nature, more and more Americans are investing in foreign companies. Many overseas markets have risen even faster than the U.S. stock markets over the years. One of the most important reasons for investing abroad is diversification. If you're interested in investing in foreign stocks, you can buy into the companies in the form of *American Depository Receipts*, or *ADRs*.

ADRs are a receipt for the shares of a foreign-based corporation held in the vault of a U.S. bank and entitling the shareholder to all dividends and capital gains. One of the nice features of owning ADRs is that the bank eliminates a lot of the inconveniences involved in owning foreign shares, including issuing dividends in American dollars and handling such matters as stock splits. ADRs generally trade over the counter, though few are listed on the New York Stock Exchange.

The greatest risk involved in foreign securities ownership is the currency risk. Foreign currency fluctuations may cut into any stock gains you may have. Additionally, it is sometimes hard to evaluate foreign companies because of different accounting standards. Information is not as quickly available as it is for U.S. stocks. To eliminate these potential problems, you may want to consider purchasing stock of foreign companies through mutual funds that specialize in foreign stocks.

What Happens If A Company Goes Bankrupt?

In the case of bankruptcy, owners of stock have the right to share in the proceeds of liquidation of assets of the corporation. Common stockholders' rights are junior to other security holders in the same company. Junior means that common stockholders' rights are satisfied after other debts of the corporation are paid.

Taxes owed to the government are the first item that gets paid with the sale of asset proceeds. After taxes, the order of liquidation is as follows: wages, senior lienholders, bank loans, subordinated debentures, preferred stock and finally common stockholders.

Investment Guides for Improved Stock Market Performance

If you are going to involve yourself in the stock market — more specifically, the *individual* stock market — you need to make sure you follow some guidelines to assure you will not lose all of your money. Investing in individual stocks is not risky if you apply some basic rules of investing.

The most important concept in successful stock investing is that return *of* your money is much more important than return *on* your money. You need to remember that preserving your money should always precede capital appreciation.

Do not average a losing stock position once the market has proven you wrong. In other words, if the market has pushed the value of your stock down, most often it is telling you that something is wrong. Do not add to a losing position.

Do not bottom-fish. Remember that many support levels are usually broken during a primary downtrend, and support often proves to be a way station to lower prices.

Always know your stock's support level. This is the price where an investor should normally cut his or her losses. Support levels help take the emotion out of investing.

Do not be afraid to take losses. Do everything possible to keep them manageable. It is important to define the point at which you will sell your stock if it starts to fall. This is a method that will keep you from losing all your money.

Do not shun a stock simply because of its price. You are far better off buying a higher-priced stock that rises in price than owning a lower-priced stock which declines in price.

Do not sell a stock solely because it seems high-priced. Let your profits run!

Once you've decided to sell a stock, you're usually best off doing so at the market. While you may get that extra ⅛ or ¼ nine times out of ten, the one time you don't can prove very costly.

Finally, *be flexible and disciplined at all times!*

The chart on the opposite page demonstrates the benefits of long-term investing. As you can see, stocks have outperformed long-term government bonds, treasury bills and inflation. Small stocks are the more growth-oriented companies, and common stocks are the blue-chip, big-name firms.

Not only have stocks outperformed these other types of investments; they have outperformed them significantly! You will notice that stocks do not go up 100% of the time. But they do go up *most* of the time.

There have always been periods when the stock market has declined temporarily. I am certain that history will repeat itself; the market will temporarily decline in years to come. But as a long-term investor, you should be concerned with 10, 15 and 20 years down the road. And as history has shown, the stock market has a very high probability of going up in the future.

Benefits of Long-Term Investing

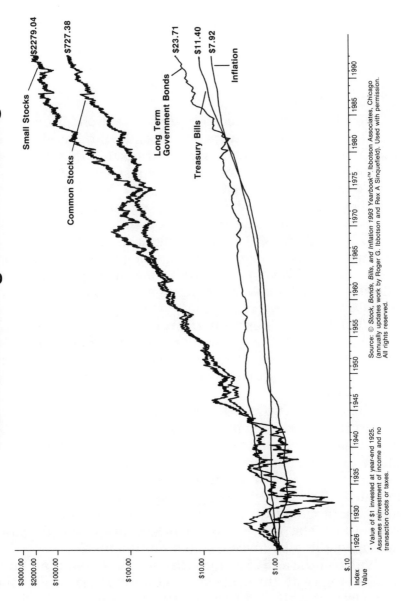

Small Stocks $2279.04

Common Stocks

$727.38

Long Term
Government Bonds $23.71

Treasury Bills $11.40

$7.92

Inflation

Index
Value

* Value of $1 invested at year-end 1925.
Assumes reinvestment of income and no
transaction costs or taxes.

Source: © Stock, Bonds, Bills, and Inflation 1993 Yearbook™ Ibbotson Associates, Chicago
(annually updates work by Roger G. Ibbotson and Rex A Sinquefield). Used with permission.
All rights reserved.

Chapter 5: Mutual Funds

How many hours of sleep have you lost wondering what is going to happen to the stock you recently purchased ... when the quote in today's paper showed it down 25%? How many nights have you lain awake second-guessing your decision to buy or sell a stock? When should I buy? When should I sell? Are they going bankrupt? Will I lose my money?

Questions like these are normal.

If these kinds of decisions make you uncomfortable, an alternative choice for your savings might be to invest in a mutual fund. This type of professional money management allows you to own different types of investments while reducing risk through diversification.

What is professional management? Professional money management is nothing more than a fund manager who takes the money you've invested and makes buy and sell decisions on your behalf. Most money managers work for mutual fund companies.

There are two ways to invest your money with professional money managers. One is by investing in a managed account where the money managers require a minimum of $100,000. These money managers do not charge a fee initially when you put your money in or when you take it out. Rather, you pay as you go. The money managers typically charge a management fee ranging from 1% to 3% of the portolio's total assets each year. The other way to attain professional money management is by investing in a mutual fund.

With as little as $250 or less in some cases, you can invest your savings with the same kind of diversification and money management with a lot less money. With a mutual fund, you have the same access to money management as people with larger sums of money.

Mutual Funds

Purchasing a mutual fund is an excellent alternative for investors who lack the time or expertise to manage their own diversified portfolio of investments. A mutual fund is simply a way for many people with different amounts of available cash to pool their money to gain professional management in exchange for a fee.

For example, let's say you have $10,000 to invest and want to buy stocks for growth. Alone, with $10,000, you can't obtain proper diversification with individual common stocks. Moreover, by buying individual stocks you would need to make your own buy and sell decisions.

But let's say that there are also 99 other people in a similar situation with $10,000 to invest. If you and the other 99 pool your money, together you have $1 million. With that $1 million, you'd have enough money to properly spread yourself among different stocks and industries. You'd also be able to hire some of the best money managers to monitor your investments.

That's what a mutual fund is. It's simply pooling your money with funds from other people with similar goals, then giving the money to a professional money manager who will properly diversify your holdings.

A mutual fund can encompass almost any kind of investment. For example, if a mutual fund has 75 stocks in it, your $10,000 includes ownership of a small piece of every one of the 75 stocks. If something happened to one of the 75 companies in the fund, it wouldn't affect your money much; remember, 74 other companies are holding up the value of your mutual fund.

The mutual fund industry has been around for a long time. The first mutual fund in the U.S. was created back in the early 1920s. But the concept didn't really take off until the 1970s. It virtually exploded throughout the 1980s and early 1990s.

In response to this demand for professional money management, there are now more than 3,500 mutual funds. They cover many different objectives and risk levels. Some mutual funds specialize in mature blue-chip stocks; others in riskier, fast-growing companies. Some funds emphasize income, while others aim for growth.

Specialized funds allow you to concentrate on specific areas of the economy. Some funds emphasize short-term money markets; others own long-term bonds. There are about as many different fund objective categories as there are days in the month. Your goal is to find the fund or funds that specifically meet your individual goals and needs.

There are two basic types of mutual funds: *open-end* and *closed-end* mutual funds.

Open-End Funds

Open-end mutual funds are by far the most popular type of mutual fund. These funds can issue an unlimited number of shares so their *size will change* as people send in money to invest or take money out. If a great many people one day decide to add money to their fund, they'd send their cash to the fund, where the manager would take that money and use it to add to the size of the fund.

Conversely, if a number of people decided simultaneously to sell some of their mutual fund, the mutual fund company would sell a portion of its investments, thereby making its size smaller, with fewer shares outstanding. Thus, the number of shares held by the fund continuously increases or decreases, based directly on share sales and redemptions.

Closed-End Funds

Closed-end mutual funds have a fixed, limited number of shares outstanding. When you purchase shares in a closed-end fund, the seller is a fellow investor, rather the fund itself as with the open-end funds. When you sell shares of your closed-end fund, the buyer is another investor and not the fund.

The closed-end fund shares trade on an exchange or over-the-counter as a stock does. You can purchase these funds through your broker, who will charge you a commission that is roughly standard for any listed security.

How Fund Shares Are Priced

The *open-end* fund figures out the total value of its portfolio of investments and divides that value by the number of fund shares outstanding. The result is the price of one share in the fund, known as the *net asset value* (NAV). The NAV is the value of each share you own in that mutual fund.

To determine the current value of your mutual fund investment, simply find the NAV in the paper and multiply it by the number of shares you hold in the fund. The result is the current value of your mutual fund holdings. The NAV is calculated daily by most funds after the close of the exchanges.

If you buy a load mutual fund, you must be aware of the *public offering price* (POP). The POP reflects the price you pay to buy the shares, including the commission. The sales charge is added to the NAV to arrive at the offering price. In a no-load fund, the offering price (POP) is the same as the net asset value (NAV) because there is no sales charge.

Closed-end fund share prices change differently. They still have a per-share net asset value, but the fund's shares don't always trade at that value. Its shares are priced by the forces of supply and demand in the open marketplace.

When buyers are abundant, the share price will rise above, or at a *premium* to, the net asset value. When sellers predominate, the price will decline and each share will sell at a *discount* from the net asset value. If the value of the investments in the fund rise or fall, so will the net asset value, just as the open-ended funds do. But because of the supply/demand nature of these funds, you can increase your profits or losses based on how far the fund trades at a discount or premium.

No-Load Mutual Funds

Some mutual funds do not have a sales charge. They are referred to as *no-load* mutual funds. You do not pay a fee to buy or sell shares in these funds.

But note: *No-load does not mean "no cost." Every mutual*

fund, regardless of whether it's load or no-load, is going to charge you something — expenses and fees — for managing your money.

No-load funds are sold directly through the mail and through newspaper, radio and television advertising. You will not have the help of a financial consultant to match your objective with a fund's objective. You, all on your own, must select the professional money managers, monitor the fund's performance, time your buys and sells, and make sure the fund is meeting your original objectives. All decisions rest in your hands.

With a no-load mutual fund you may invest, for example, $10,000. All that money goes to work for you immediately. That's one of its advantages. You do not pay a fee to get in or out of the fund. The disadvantage is the lack of help in making decisions.

Of course, like any other mutual fund, the no-load funds have annual management fees that are taken out of the fund assets.

Load Mutual Funds

Load mutual funds charge a fee for purchasing shares in the fund. This load is a fee paid to the financial consultant for his or her advice. The load can range anywhere from 1% to a legal maximum of 8.5%. Most load funds have a fee ranging from 3% to 6%. Generally, once you've paid your initial fee, there will be no additional fees when you sell the fund. In the newspaper, this fee is reflected in the difference between the net asset value and the public offering price.

Some funds charge no commissions when you buy, but may charge a fee when you sell the fund, depending on the length of time you hold it. Generally the amount of the fee will decline as you hold the fund shares for a longer period of time. This is called a *redemption fee* (back-end load). Eventually (usually after five years) you can sell the fund without a fee.

Most load mutual funds reduce the sales charge when you invest large amounts of money within their family. These fee discounts are called *break points*. A break point is a dollar investment that is required to make the fundholder eligible for a lower sales charge. For example, if you had $10,000 to invest, the sales charge might be 5%; but if you had $50,000 to invest within a family, the fund may only charge a fee of 3.75%. Different funds structure their break points at different levels. Some may start out at $25,000, while others begin at $50,000 to $100,000.

You don't necessarily have to have all of the $50,000 in hand at once to reach the break point. If you plan on reaching the break point within (usually) 13 months, the funds generally allow you to take advantage of these lower sales charges right from the beginning. If you do sign a *letter of intent* saying you're going to meet the minimum break point but don't actually make it within the required 13 months, the fund will charge you the fees you should have paid based on the lesser amount.

In addition to the fee, like any other mutual fund, the fund will deduct an annual management fee from the fund's assets.

Fees and Expenses

All mutual funds, whether they're load or no-load, charge internal management fees. These fees cover a variety of expenses, including the portfolio manager's salary, research expenses and computer, and mailing costs. These management fees normally range anywhere from ½% to 2% percent annually, depending on the fund's objective. There may also be a fee that pays for advertising and marketing expenses; it is called a *12-b 1 fee.*

Mutual funds that are more aggressive in buying and selling, such as growth mutual funds, naturally have higher management expenses than those that invest in bonds.

When purchasing a mutual fund, watch to make sure that the fund's management expenses are in line with others in its own category. Some funds charge excessive fees to pay for advertising and other related costs. These excessive fees ultimately eat into the fund's annual profits.

One place these fees can be found is in the mutual fund's *prospectus.* A prospectus is a legal document that describes the fund's objective, its management, and its charges and expenses and other essential data.

Load vs No-Load Debate

Which group of funds, load or no-load, is more appropriate for me? How do I evaluate the merits of a load versus a no-load mutual fund? Is one better than the other? Load considerations need to be put into proper context before its merits can be evaluated.

The following is a comment from the highly respected mutual fund rating agency *Morningstar* on the debate on load vs no-load mutual funds.

"On one hand, it would be wrong to ignore the fees, since they clearly impact real-world returns to investors. On the other hand, to consider their full penalties over a short-term time horizon of say, one year, when the holding period is substantially longer also seems wrong. Placing load considerations in their proper context is clearly an important matter.

"Ironically, the debate over the relative merits of load and no-load funds has intensified even as the differences between the two camps have grown more blurred. In recent years, some full-load fund families have cut back their front-end fees, while some formerly no-load groups have attached front-end fees to some of their funds.

"Despite the difficulty of defining load and no-load funds, a number of industry commentators continue to make unsubstantiated opinions that investors should only buy no-load funds. While no-load funds may be a better option for some investors, the conclusion that they are the best option for all investors is misguided. For one thing, such thinking eliminates a number of the best portfolio managers in the world, from one's choices. To start a mutual fund search by eliminating many top managers is hardly a promising course of action. A better way to proceed is to try to separate good funds from bad ones. After all, an investor is clearly far better off in a good load fund than in a bad no-load one.

"A sales fee is just one of many considerations an investor

must evaluate in appraising a fund. To place too great a weighting on this, or any other single variable, can cause investors to unduly neglect other investment considerations, such as risk levels, managerial ability, and portfolio strategy. Successful investing requires a balanced approach.

"A fund's sales fee must be placed in proper context for effective evaluation. If an investor's personal time horizon is relatively short, say two or three years, then load considerations should be given greater priority than would be the case if a ten year holding period were anticipated.

"Even more important than considering the effect of a sales fee, however, is to consider the relative gain an investor can receive from paying such fees. A load generally represents a payment for advisory services given by the financial consultant who sells the fund. If an investor receives good advice, these fees can be a tremendous bargain. The danger, of course, is that an investor may pay the same fee to an uninformed consultant that is paid to a dedicated financial consultant.

"Fees are well-spent money for investors working with a good financial consultant. Furthermore, because consultants receive no additional fees for moving an investor within a fund family, there is less incentive to rapidly buy and sell a load-fund account. Not surprisingly, load funds typically report longer average shareholder holding periods than do no-load funds. Accordingly, load funds may actually help enforce long-term thinking, while no-loads create greater potential for whipsaw.

"We are not suggesting that investors should only consider load funds. But with all the load-fund bashing of recent years, we think it's important to recognize that these funds do have substantial benefits and that no-load funds are not the perfect answer for all investors. To divide the industry across such simple barriers not only flies in the face of the growing reality of mid-load funds, but it generates a great deal of misleading advice and unfairly discredits the work of many fine financial consultants."

The question: Which is best for you? The answer is, "It depends."

If you have the time, expertise, resources and ability to

sleep at night, and if you enjoy picking your own mutual funds out of the more than 3,500 available, then perhaps a no-load mutual fund is most appropriate.

If, however, you need help finding the fund most appropriate for your needs and don't have the time, expertise or resources to do your own homework, then a load mutual fund might be the perfect answer. If you feel you need investment counsel, it makes sense to buy a load fund.

Interestingly, studies show that there is no correlation between a fund's performance and whether or not you pay a fee to buy it.

How a Mutual Fund Works

A mutual fund can make money for investors in several ways. One is through *dividends* and *interest* earned on its investments. The dividends and interest are passed on to the shareholders. They are treated as taxable income for that year, just as any interest from other investments would be. The earnings can be paid monthly or quarterly, depending on which type of mutual fund you own.

If the mutual fund manager decides to sell an investment within the fund for a profit, the profit would be passed on to you in the form of a *capital gain.* A capital gain is the profit of the investment sold within the fund. These gains are usually paid semiannually or annually.

You don't have to take these dividends, interest and capital gains in cash. In fact, unless you really need the money, I recommend you reinvest any distributions you receive in the purchase of additional shares of the fund. This can be done very easily by indicating on the account application that you wish to reinvest all dividends and capital gains. Additionally, most funds allow you to reinvest these dividends and capital gains without paying a fee on the reinvested shares.

Benefits of Mutual Funds

One important benefit of mutual funds is *diversification.* Diversification allows you to spread your risk among different investments. Let's say you owned a mutual fund that has 100 stocks in its portfolio and one of the 100 companies within the fund went bankrupt. It really isn't going to affect your investment very much because your fund has 99 other stocks holding up its value. If you had owned the one stock that went bankrupt, however, you would have lost all your money.

Another benefit is *convenience*. Some mutual funds allow investors to start out with minimum investments as small as $100. This gives small investors the ability to take advantage of the same kind of investments as people with larger amounts. In addition, you normally have the privilege of automatically reinvesting both dividends and capital gains without fees. This enables you to speed up your compounding potential and eliminates your decision on what to do with the dividend checks.

Having professionals do your *record-keeping* is a tremendous benefit of mutual funds. You have the choice of taking the dividends or capital gains in cash or reinvesting them. You simply make your choice when you open the account; the fund takes care of the rest. At the end of the year, the fund will provide you with a year-end summary of all transactions. Additionally, at year-end the fund will provide you with tax information regarding your distributions.

Investing in mutual funds allows you to do all the things you want, without the worry of making buy and sell decisions. Instead of staying home analyzing your investments, losing sleep, or wondering if you're going to lose your money, you can be out golfing or sitting at the lake getting a suntan or catching a walleye.

What To Look For in Mutual Funds

One of the things you must look for in mutual funds is their *performance relative to other funds with the same objective*. One cannot simply say, "Because I earned 13% a year for the last ten years, I had a good stock fund." If you earned 13% a year during the decade of the 1980s, you underperformed the stock fund averages. You should have earned around 15%–17% a year. That's what the average stock fund did

did during the 1980s. Thirteen percent per year is only good if the other funds in the same category did 13% a year.

What I'm saying is that without doing a mutual fund evaluation, you cannot be sure if the fund you're about to buy or the fund you currently own is doing well relative to others in its own category. Earning 13% a year sounds good until you find out that your friends and peers owned a fund that returned 17% and shares the same objective and risk level as yours!

On the other side of the coin, don't feel bad if one of your funds didn't do as well as your neighbor's. One reason your neighbor's fund may have outperformed yours may be that his or her fund has a higher risk level. You may have owned a conservative growth-and-income fund that averaged 15% a year. This may have been right in line with expectations, while your neighbor averaged 17% a year with a more aggressive growth mutual fund. That's reasonable; the more aggressive fund has a higher risk level and *should* have a higher return. It's not fair to compare the two. *You should only compare your fund with other funds that have the same objectives and risk levels.*

Because many funds look alike and are similar within their own objective, it is important to find a fund that has superior management. For example, most growth funds own similar stocks. So what separates one fund from the other? In other words, if most funds generally own the same stocks, how could one fund outperform another? The answer is *management style.*

Management performance is arguably the most important single variable determining which fund performs the most consistently year after year. Some funds use a star management style; this is where one person, and one person only, calls the shots. Other funds use committee-style management where a number of people together make decisions on behalf of the fund.

One way to determine a manager's style is to look at turnover. The turnover ratio will tell you how often the investments within the fund are being bought and sold. Does the fund have a high turnover, or is management using a buy-and-hold strategy with low turnover? Does the fund have high or low internal expenses?

Internal expenses, turnover ratio and management structure all contribute to defining the fund's management style. As a conservative investor, it is very important that you find a style that you understand and are comfortable with. *Consistency through good markets and bad markets is the key!*

One thing you want to avoid is choosing the hottest fund of the moment. Funds that do spectacularly well when the market is rising often do spectacularly badly when it begins to fall. In short, this year's heroes can easily turn into next year's bums.

It is wise to look for funds that have been consistently profitable over the years, those that have outperformed the broad stock indexes in both *up* and *down* market cycles. This provides the best test of fund managers' ability to handle money over the long term.

Chapter 6: Retirement Plans

Individual Retirement Accounts

The Individual Retirement Account (IRA) might just be the best thing that ever happened to you. The IRA is everyone's retirement plan. It doesn't matter if you are young or old, involved in a retirement plan or not ... almost everyone with earned income can contribute money to an IRA each year.

First, let's define what an IRA *isn't.* An IRA is *not* an investment. Many savers in the 1970s and 1980s simply walked into a bank and "bought" an IRA. Most people didn't realize that their IRA money was being invested in CDs. That's why IRAs showed such good returns in the early 1980s. Because investors didn't realize that they did have investment alternatives available, the misperception developed that an IRA is an investment.

An IRA is a form of retirement account. Within this retirement account you can put your money into any type of investment you choose — a stock, bond, mutual fund or other investment vehicle.

The IRA was created in 1974 as part of the Employee Retirement Income Security Act (ERISA). Most of the growth, however, came in the 1980s when the Economic Recovery Tax Act of 1981 expanded both the amount and the eligibility of IRA accounts. The liberalization of IRAs was considered an admission by Congress that adequate Social Security may not be there when today's younger adults are ready for it or that it may be in ailing health, so they encouraged Americans to build up their retirement saving outside of Social Security. This act extended the $2,000 deductible contribution to everyone, including those participating in company-sponsored retirement plans, as long as they had at least an equal amount in earned income.

But then along came our lawmakers with the Tax Reform Act of '86. Surprisingly, the act phased out the deductions on IRAs for a large number of individuals. Along with it went the incentive to save using an IRA.

Who is eligible for the deduction?

Eligibility depends on two things: income and participation in a company-sponsored retirement plan.

Employed people and their spouses, single filers or joint filers who are not covered by a pension plan can deduct all contributions to an IRA regardless of income.

If either you or your spouse are involved in a company retirement plan, then your deductibility will be phased out based on your adjusted gross income (AGI). Married couples who file jointly can deduct their full IRA deposits if their AGI is $40,000 or less per year, regardless of whether either spouse participates in a pension plan. If one of you does participate in a pension plan and your AGI is between $40,000 and $50,000, then a portion of your contribution is deductible. When you make more than $50,000 AGI, your deductibility has been totally phased out.

Single filers can deduct up to $2,000 if they earn $25,000 or less, regardless of pension plan status. If a single filer's AGI is between $25,000 and $35,000 and he or she is involved in a pension plan, then only a portion is deductible. After $35,000 AGI, the deductibility has been phased out.

Even if only one of you is involved in a plan, you are out of luck. Your deductibility is phased out based on your adjusted gross income. But remember, deductibility is not the same as a contribution. As long as you have earned income, you may contribute up to $2,000 to an IRA regardless of your pension plan status; the problem is only that the $2,000 may not be deductible.

When can I contribute to my IRA?

You can contribute to your IRA any time during the year up to April 15 of the following year. In other words, Uncle Sam will give you a 3½–month grace period to make your contributions. For example, if you want to make a 1993 IRA contribution, you can contribute at any time during the year 1993 up to your tax-filing deadline, usually April 15 of the following year (1994).

One alternative to funding your contribution with a single lump sum of $2,000 is to contribute on a systematic basis. It may be easier to fund your IRA in 12 monthly installments of $166. This will not only make it easier to afford, but also will force you to save for your future. Make your IRA part of your budgeting obligations like your car or house. It makes saving much easier.

If you can't afford $2,000 at tax time or $166 per month, fund what you can afford, even if it's $250 or $500. Something is better than nothing. It's your retirement we are talking about.

What are the IRA age limits?

You may contribute to an IRA as long as you are at least one day old and can continue until you've reached 70½, as long as you have earned income. Once you've reached the government's golden age of 70½, they feel you should be reaping the fruits of your labor. They no longer allow contributions to your IRA anymore; in fact, they force you to start taking mandatory distributions from your IRA at that age.

Even children can fund IRAs. Children who have paper routes or work summer jobs can — and do — have IRAs. How could someone months old have an IRA? Have you ever seen those babies on TV commercials? The infants who work as models do earn income; a tax return is filed on their behalf, and hence, they are eligible to set up an IRA!

Spousal IRAs

An individual can set up an IRA for his or her non-working spouse under certain conditions. The spouse must have no compensation for the year, and a joint tax return must be filed. The law says the two accounts can be funded to a maximum of $2,250 per year. That is, the total contribution for both accounts cannot exceed $2,250.

You can split up the money any way you wish, provided that not more than $2,000 goes into either account in a given year. You can put $1,125 in each account, or only $250 in your account and $2,000 in your spouse's account. But remember, you can't own IRAs jointly. The IRAs must be kept separate.

The deductibility of the contribution is still based on the restrictions listed for combined joint income. Interestingly, you can contribute the full $2,000 to your spouse's IRA based on your earnings even if you are over 70½ years old, as long as your spouse is under 70½.

Where Can I Invest My IRA Money?

Let's first talk about where you *can't* invest your IRA money. You can't hold *collectibles* in an IRA, such as precious metals (gold, silver or platinum), gems, coins, rugs, artwork, antiques, Elvis memorabilia or postage stamps. There is one exception, however; you can invest in certain gold or silver coins minted by the U.S. Treasury or the states, such as the American Eagle gold coin. Life insurance is also forbidden.

You *can* invest your money in an IRA in various places. You have your choice ranging from individual stocks to bonds, CDs or mutual funds. But first, you are going to need a custodian or trustee — a bank, savings and loan, or approved custodian such as a mutual fund or brokerage firm. By the way, you *cannot* pledge the IRA as security for a loan as you can some retirement accounts.

Within these trustee choices, you have a lot of flexibility to invest your IRA money. If you feel you need to have your IRA insured by the federal government, you can put it into a CD or money market deposit account in a bank or S&L where it will earn guaranteed interest. If you want to own only mutual funds, you can choose to open an IRA account at a mutual fund company and have your money invested in its fund family.

If you want to diversify your IRA money within one account where you might own a combination of stocks, bonds, mutual funds and CDs, you would need to open a *self-directed* IRA at a stock brokerage firm. The self-directed IRA gives you the flexibility to diversify all your investments within one IRA.

Just because you have all of those investment options available doesn't mean you have to invest in them. First and foremost, you must be able to sleep at night with the investments within your IRA. Second, you should have your IRA money properly diversified to meet your own specific objectives, risk tolerance and goals.

For a younger person that might mean keeping a larger percentage of money in the growth area (stocks). A retired person might have less money in individual stocks and more in the income area, such as in CDs or bonds. Take a look at your individual situation and decide for yourself what you're looking for and where you are trying to go with your IRA money.

IRA Withdrawals

The government will allow you to contribute money to an IRA for a maximum of 70½ years. That should give you plenty of time to build a nice nest egg. But at the same time, in return for allowing you to defer paying taxes for that long, the government wants to make sure that at some point you will have to pay the taxes you legally postponed.

By April 1 of the year *after* you reach 70½, you must start withdrawing money from your IRA. The amount you are required to withdraw each year is governed by your life expectancy. The government takes the number of years you're expected to live, then divides that number into all the tax-deferred assets you have. The total is the minimum annual distribution. If you have more than one IRA, all accounts must be totalled together to get the minimum distribution; however, you can take that distribution from just one of the IRAs. All the government cares is that you take out the minimum amount.

You don't have to wait until you are 70½ to withdraw money from your IRA. You may start taking distributions at any time in any amount after you reach the age of 59½. If you withdraw funds from your IRA before you reach the age of 59½ you will not only be required to pay taxes on that money, but you will also pay a stiff early withdrawal penalty of 10%. (There are a few exceptions, like disability.)

When you open your IRA account, you must designate a beneficiary. When you die, the money from the IRA goes to the beneficiary you've named. A spouse may re-register the IRA in his or her name and continue enjoying tax deferral. If your beneficiary is not your spouse, the money must be withdrawn and the tax paid in no more than five annual installments.

How do I move from one IRA to another IRA?

There are two ways to move your money from one IRA account to another. You can either *transfer* it or *roll it over*.

When you *transfer* your IRA, you are having your IRA assets sent directly from one custodian to a new custodian. In this case you will not take possession of the money; rather, it will be directly transferred from custodian to custodian. Because the money is transferred directly, there is no reporting done to the IRS. This is the cleanest way to move your IRA. Moreover, there is no limit to the number of transfers you can do per year.

The other way to move your money from one IRA to another is to do a *roll-over*. When you roll over an IRA, you take possession of the IRA assets and are given up to 60 days to deposit those assets with a new IRA custodian. If you don't reinvest the money in another IRA within the 60-day limit, the government will make you pay ordinary income taxes on all of the money not rolled over. Additionally, if you are under 59½, you may also have to pay a 10% early withdrawal penalty.

Note: *The newly created 20% withholding rule does not apply to distributions from IRAs or SEPs.* It only applies to qualified retirement plans.

You are allowed *only one* IRA-to-IRA rollover per year in which the money is available for 60-day spending.

Don't let the complexity of the IRA rules get you down and keep you from contributing to an IRA. The benefits of tax deferral and compounding make it an excellent vehicle for retirement planning. Its only real negative is the limitation on how much you can contribute or deduct each year.

If you feel overwhelmed by rules and regulations, go see a financial consultant for help. That's what he or she is paid for.

Should I consolidate my IRAs?

The answer is, *it depends*. It depends on where the money is coming from. Because banks in the early 1980s were paying a high rate of interest on their CDs in IRAs, it was common for people to shop around each year to find out whose IRA paid the highest rate. When they found that rate, they simply opened an IRA at the new bank.

This kind of thing happened year after year while interest rates were high. So here we are today with multiple IRAs. In fact, many people have as many as five or more IRAs scattered around earning different rates at different places. This can be unfortunate; when investors have numerous IRAs on every street corner, many don't have a good handle on how well they are doing, when they come due, and each IRA's value.

By consolidating these IRAs you can gain three distinct advantages. One: Your money is easier to manage. You can see on one statement how well your IRA investments are doing. Two: Your custodial costs should be lower. You will be paying one fee instead of several. Three: It is easier to keep track of investments within the IRAs. It's also easier to diversify within one account because you can get a bird's eye view of each investment's individual status at one glance.

There is one exception to consolidation: If your money is coming from a qualified retirement plan and going into an IRA, you should create a second IRA account or *roll-over* IRA account. Keep it separate from the traditional account to which you have been contributing annually. This is wise because you may be able to deposit your old retirement money into your new employer's retirement plan. If you choose to go to work for another company with a retirement plan that accepts roll-over contributions, you will still have the option of taking this roll-over IRA money from your previous plan and putting it into your new company's retirement plan.

If, on the other hand, you have rolled over all of your traditional IRAs and your qualified IRA into one account, you will never be able to move that money to a qualified plan again. Once they've all been consolidated into one account, it's too late. The process can't be reversed.

On still another hand, if you are positive that you are retiring for good and won't acquire a new qualified plan in the future, there's no need to create two different IRAs. In that case, it makes more sense to consolidate.

Should I roll over or transfer my company retirement plan?

Before January 1, 1993, you were able to take a distribution from your qualified retirement plan when you retired or quit your job. You could take possession of that money for a short period of time — 60 days — before transferring it to another IRA or retirement plan custodian.

In late 1992, the government decided that because the money was earmarked for retirement, there is no reason you should be able to take the money out of the IRA for two months and use it as you please before finally rolling it over. They decided that if you take possession of the qualified money for even one day, you will be subject to *mandatory 20% income-tax withholding.*

Under the new rules, all eligible roll-over distributions from qualified retirement plans are subject to this 20% withholding tax unless there is a *direct roll-over* into an IRA or other retirement plan. A direct roll-over can be accomplished by having the check written out directly to the new trustee or custodian of the new IRA or retirement plan.

Congress did not eliminate the 60-day requirement for roll-overs. Consequently, if you do not elect a direct roll-over or transfer of the distribution (thus avoiding the 20% withholding), you will only be able to achieve a tax-free rollover of 80% of the distribution within the 60-day period. The only way to avoid taxation of that 20% withholding is to deposit the 20% out of your own pocket at the same time as the roll-over. This tactic entitles you to a tax-free refund of the 20% withheld at tax time.

For example, let's say you left ABC Corporation with $100,000 in the retirement plan. Under the old rules, you could receive a check for $100,000 and complete a tax-free rollover to an IRA within 60 days. Under the new rules, you will receive a check for $80,000, while $20,000 (or 20%) is withheld and sent to the IRS. There are two ways to avoid this:

1) You may add $20,000 out of your own pocket to your

$80,000 and rollover $100,000 to the IRA or retirement plan. Then you could claim a refund of $20,000 when you file your taxes. If you don't add to your distribution, the IRS will tax the $20,000 withheld as ordinary income and impose a 10% premature penalty tax if you're are under age 59½.

2) Don't take the distribution until you have arranged a direct roll-over or transfer into an IRA or new qualified plan.

Essentially, what the government is saying is that you should directly roll over or transfer your qualified money to another retirement plan or IRA rather than take possession of it. In this way you will eliminate the 20% mandatory income-tax withholding.

Annuities

Just the mention of the term *annuity* can make some people weak at the knees. Annuities can be described as a way to build savings for a future need, or can be described as the opposite of life insurance. While life insurance helps to create an estate, annuities amortize the estate.

An *annuity* is simply an agreement, generally between an insurance company and an individual, through which the individual pays a given sum (in a lump-sum payment or a series of regular payments) in return for some future income received in one or more payments annually for a certain period of time or for life.

You can choose to have the insurance company start paying a regular monthly check immediately by *annuitizing*. Or you can allow the insurance company to invest your money, and then begin receiving your monthly checks at some point in the future.

Annuities may be classified as *fixed* or *variable*. A fixed annuity will pay a fixed number of dollars to the owner. A variable annuity will base its payments to the owner on the performance of its investment portfolio. In a variable annuity, payments may vary from month to month, while payments in a fixed annuity are always the same.

When you invest in a *fixed annuity,* you will know the *floor* (the minimum you'll earn) for the life of the contract. But for a certain period — usually one, three or five years — you'll be guaranteed a fixed rate of interest, possibly more than the floor.

The major advantage of a fixed annuity is that you'll know exactly what you are going to earn for exactly how long. The contract value will not fluctuate with market conditions as the variable annuity does. Fixed annuities are considered insurance products, not securities. A variable annuity, on the other hand, is considered to be a security under federal securities laws.

Variable annuities appeal to people who want the opportunity for higher returns that may come from assuming higher risks. With a variable annuity, there is no guaranteed rate of return. In this annuity, the insurance company offers as investment options any number of diversified securities such as stocks, bonds or other securities. You determine how much of your money will be allocated to each of the areas offered. You have the freedom to switch between investments such as stocks, money markets and bond portfolios without a charge or tax liability.

The value of your variable annuity changes with general market conditions. If you had your money invested in the stock option, and stocks go up, the value of your account goes up and vice versa.

The objectives of investing in variable annuities are to provide a hedge against expected long-term inflation, to increase annuity income by participating in the appreciative values and dividends of common stocks, and to provide a steady increase in living standards. The values of the common stocks are expected to rise more than the cost of living over the long run. Thus, variable annuities are expected to preserve and to increase real retirement income.

Although they are sold by insurance companies and considered life insurance contracts, variable annuities are not life insurance policies. They are legally defined as securities because the issuer does not assume the investment risk.

Comparing Fixed and Variable Annuities

The central difference between fixed and variable annuities is the payout. With a fixed annuity, the annuitant is paid the same amount during each payout period, reflecting the relatively stable portfolio of bonds and mortgages. With a variable annuity, the annuitant is paid a variable amount that reflects the performance of the portfolio of stocks and bonds.

Before selecting one of the two types of annuities, first determine your financial condition and needs. The advantage of the fixed annuity is that you'll know exactly how much you are going to get. The disadvantage is the purchasing power risk — the risk that the fixed payout's purchasing power will be eroded during periods of inflation.

Because you can select stocks in the variable annuity, the amount of payouts may increase during periods of inflation, helping to maintain your purchasing power. The disadvantage is that a declining market could decrease the variable annuity's value, and thus risk the loss of principal.

Types of Annuities

There are two basic types of annuities: *immediate* and *deferred.* Let's look at the two and their differences.

If you decide you want to supplement your retirement income and want that supplement to start immediately, you may choose the *immediate* annuity contract. You put in a lump sum of money; then payments begin. If the contract is for monthly payments, they begin one month after the date of purchase. If the contract calls for annual payments, payments begin one year after the date of purchase.

The idea is that you will never run out of money during your lifetime. You give the insurance company your money, and they tell you how much they can pay you monthly. The monthly amount depends on your age and the amount you are depositing, plus the amount the insurance company figures it can earn with your money minus its expenses. The appealing part of this type of annuity is that it can be used as a form of systematic liquidation of principal and interest over your lifetime.

Maybe you've decided that you don't need immediate income from your investments. You do want to take advantage of the tax deferral feature of annuities and build up more money before you start taking payments. In this case, you might consider a *deferred* annuity.

When you purchase a deferred annuity, you choose your investment option for the annuity — either fixed or variable — and your money grows tax deferred until you decide to take it out. In other words, your money will grow as it does in your IRA or company retirement plan. However, your investment is not tax deductible unless the annuity is in an IRA. Taxes are deferred only on your earnings.

You should not use these annuities for emergency money. Even though the tax deferral looks good, if you need to take your money out of the annuity before you reach the age of 59½, you will be charged a 10% penalty plus ordinary income taxes on the amount that represents the withdrawal of interest.

Moreover, the insurance company may assess a fee called a *surrender charge*. If you take out your money after the first few years, the company may charge you a substantial fee for pulling it out early. These surrender charges are intended to make up for the fee that was paid to the salesperson who sold you your annuity. Surrender charges decline as years go by, until at some point — usually five or six years — they are gone. Most companies will allow you to make penalty-free withdrawals of up to 10% of your account balance each year.

When you take money out of your annuity, the tax laws require that you first withdraw the earnings, which are taxable. The rest of your withdrawal considered the return of principal, and need not be taxed.

Payout Options

Once you've decided that you are going to spend all that money you've saved over the years, you may decide to *annuitize*. To annuitize means that you will hand over your money to the insurance company; then they will pay you income for the rest of your life.

If you decide to annuitize, you relinquish the right to control your money ever again. The insurance company has all control. It is irreversible.

You then must choose a payout option for your money. I'll cover a few of the several options available.

When you hand over your money to the insurance company to pay you income for the rest of your life, you are taking one major risk: If you die a year or so after you started taking income, then the insurance company is entitled to keep the balance of the money.

To prevent this from happening, you may want to choose a *life annuity with period-certain payout.* A life annuity with a period-certain option will make monthly or periodic payments to the annuitant for life. If you die prior to the end of the specified period, the payments will be made in a lump sum or in installments to your designated beneficiary until the end of the period-certain.

For example, Mr. Jones chooses a 10-year period-certain life annuity and dies after receiving payments for five years. The annuity company will continue to pay his named beneficiary for the remaining five years of the contract. Had Mr. Jones died after 15 years, the annuity company would have been obligated to pay up to his death. Since his death occurred five years after the end of the period certain, the annuity company would be relieved of any payments to a beneficiary.

If you want your annuity payments to be paid to two people, you would choose a *joint and last survivor life* annuity. The payout continues during the lifetime of two people, usually husband and wife. When one person dies, the survivor continues to receive only his or her payments. Upon death of the surviving beneficiary, payments will cease.

One thing to keep in mind when choosing a payout option is how much risk the insurance company is taking. The better the payout option looks to you, the lower the monthly payout will be. If you choose a payout option that only covers yourself for life, the insurance company will probably pay you a higher monthly income than if you choose a payout option that includes both you and your spouse for life. When the insurance company has to pay two, they are assuming much more risk because both or either of you might outlive your life expectancies; this eventuality would cost the insurance company more to keep paying the survivor until his or her death.

Not all insurance companies offer the same payouts. The age and sex of the annuitant are taken into consideration, as well as the current interest rate environment.

There are a few things you should consider before buying an annuity. First and foremost, you would be wise to deal with only major insurers who are rated above-average by rating agencies such as A.M. Best, Standard & Poor's and Moody's. You are giving your money to an insurance company, so it's important to check its track record. Remember, *a guarantee is only as good as the guarantor.*

Second, when shopping for a fixed annuity, don't give in to the temptation to buy the one that promises the highest rate of interest. *Many contracts show a high rate for first-time buyers for a one-year period, then slash the interest in the following years of the contract.* To prevent this from happening, you should ask the insurance company for the interest rates that they have paid in the last five to ten years. Also be sure to ask if the annuity has a *bail-out provision.*

A bail-out provision allows you to pull out your money without incurring an early-withdrawal penalty. The bail-out provision can be utilized, providing the interest rate on the annuity falls below a minimum level, such as one to two percentage points below the rate offered when you bought the annuity. If you bail out, you can move your money to another company without paying taxes. But you're generally better off with a no-bail-out annuity from a company that consistently pays high rates. The bail-out feature costs the insurance company money, and it passes those costs on to you in the form of lower interest rates.

Annuities can be a very important part of good, comprehensive financial planning. Since the features of annuities are complex, ask your financial consultant for a more detailed explanation. Remember, that's what he or she gets paid to do. Let your consultant help you sort through the annuity jungle.

Keoughs and SEPs

Before these types of retirement plans were introduced, doctors, lawyers, plumbers, electricians and all those who were self-employed were left out in the cold when it came to retirement savings. Concern for retirement provisions for self-employed individuals led to creation of the *Keough plan* in 1972. The plan is named after the congressman who introduced the bill that established it.

The purpose of the legislation that brought about the Keough plan was to eliminate the inequitable treatment of self-employed persons who could not participate in qualified pension or profit-sharing plans. An IRS-approved Keough plan allows a self-employed individual to establish a tax-deferred retirement fund. Earnings accumulate tax-free, with taxes deferred until the individual actually withdraws them, normally after age 59½ or at the time of disability.

A Keough plan must be established by someone who is self-employed, and the money funded to the plan must come from that self-employment. If you are self-employed part-time, only your earnings from self-employment may be used in calculating contributions to the Keough.

There are two types of Keough plans: *defined-contribution* and *defined-benefit* plans. Most Keough plans today are defined-contribution plans. The percentage amount that may be contributed annually is based on compensation. The annual maximum is $22,500 or 25% of compensation, whichever is less. This arrangement gives you the flexibility to make minimal or no contributions in a year in which you do not have net income. With defined-contribution, your retirement income is based on how much you have contributed and on what your Keough investments earn throughout the years.

Because *defined-benefit* Keough plans are more costly to set up and administer, they are not as popular as the defined-contribution plan. The contributions in a defined-benefit plan can vary greatly from year to year. There is no actual dollar limit. Only the size of the pension is limited.

Under the defined-benefit plan, you promise yourself a retirement benefit of some fixed amount each month for the rest of your life. Your annual contributions are based on the amount needed to provide you the size of pension you've chosen at the normal retirement age. You'll know ahead of time exactly what your Keough will be worth at retirement. This may commit your company to making a contribution no matter what the profit picture.

A Keough account must be established by December 31 of that tax year in order to be tax-deductible. Once the plan is established, future contributions may be postponed until April 15 of the following year or until the tax-filing deadline — or later, if you apply for an extended deadline.

A Simplified Employee Plan (SEP) is a hybrid of an IRA and a Keough. It is similar to a Keough in that it is funded by the employer; but like an IRA, the account is maintained solely by the employee. The SEP is available for any business owner, sole proprietor, partnership or corporation. *It is the only business retirement plan that allows a business contribution and an IRA contribution into the same plan.*

Those who must be covered under the SEP plan include the business owner and all employees 21 years of age or older who have performed service (for any length of time) during three of the last five years, and have received a minimum of $374 of compensation.

The SEP must be established by the employer's tax-filing deadline, unlike the Keough in which the account must be established by December 31. All contributions must be made by the time the employer files his or her taxes. The business owner may make annual contributions to the SEP up to 15% or $22,500 of earned income, whichever is less.

Distributions from the SEP are the same as those outlined for the IRA. If an individual is over the age of 70½, he or she must take mandatory distributions. If the individual is still employed, however, he or she still must receive a SEP contribution.

The SEP is less costly to administer than the other types of self-employed retirement plans. Each participant has his or her own account, so the employer does not have the responsibility of making investment decisions for the employees. No annual reports to the government are necessary.

Chapter 7: Asset Allocation

Asset allocation is where the rubber meets the road. You can learn all you want about individual investments, but without allocating your money to take advantage of investment opportunities and prevent major losses, your probability of investment success is severely limited.

The *benefits of asset allocation* are threefold.

First, asset allocation allows you to take advantage of current investment opportunities, thus increasing your total returns over the long haul.

Second, it prevents you from putting all your eggs in one basket, thereby reducing the chances of severe fluctuations in any given period.

Third, asset allocation positions your money relative to your risk tolerance. It allows you to maximize returns on your money relative to your ability to sleep at night.

Asset allocation is nothing more than positioning your money within the three investment areas — growth, income, and cash. The cash area includes investments like savings accounts and money markets. The income portion includes investments that have a primary objective of providing income, such as bonds and CDs. The growth area includes stocks and stock-related investments. The growth area provides you with a hedge against inflation.

Exploiting Economic Trends

Economic trends change over time, so your allocation will eventually change as well. *All markets move in cycles.* For example, as our economy comes out of a recession, cyclical stocks tend to perform better than most other stocks at that time. The growth portion of your portfolio might shift a portion of its assets to the cyclical industries to take advantage of their moves. Likewise, different industries move through their cycles at different times, so you must structure your portfolio to take advantage of their profits.

As interest rates rise and fall, your portfolio will take advantage of the interest rates being offered. It will diversify its income investment holdings to maximize current returns while still maintaining the flexibility to react to future interest rate changes.

News events affecting the market can be scary: presidents shot, bombs dropped, interest rates rising, and so on. There will be many more uncertainties in the future. It's important to remember not to panic. Throughout it all, your guiding philosophy is to maintain a long-term perspective.

You will change the allocation of your assets as market conditions — and your own personal needs — change. But even these changes should be consistent with your long-term perspective.

Reduce Fluctuation and Potential Losses

Two of the biggest benefits of asset allocation are to *reduce fluctuation* and *eliminate the potential for large losses*.

Let's look at a truly incredible statistic. Let's say you've invested your money and earned 15% each year for three straight years. In the fourth year, your portfolio lost 15%. What do you think your average annual return is after this fourth year?

This may surprise you! Let's look at the math.

Year 1	+15%
Year 2	+15%
Year 3	+15%
Year 4	−15%
Average Annual Return	+6.6%

That is what *only one bad year* will do to three great years of returns. It would take a return of +56% in the fifth year to make up for that fourth year (−15%) to get you back to an annualized +15% per year!

Here is another way to look at the effects of losses on a portfolio. Let's say you've invested $100,000; one year later, you had a loss of 20%. Your portfolio would now be worth $80,000 (20% of $100,000 = $20,000).

What would it take to get your $80,000 back to the original $100,000? More than +20%! Your money would need to earn +25% ($80,000 x 25% = $20,000) the following year ... just to break even!

The moral of the story is that if you put all your eggs in one basket, you are increasing the odds — almost guaranteeing them — of suffering one of those bad years. All the time and energy you put into the past three years can be erased in only one bad year!

If, on the other hand, you have your money properly diversified among a number of different investments that provide for safety, income and growth, the probability of suffering a big loss in any one given period is significantly reduced.

Remember, we are aiming for *consistency* year after year. Your first goal is to keep your money safe, and second, to make your money grow surely and consistently in good *and* bad years.

With proper asset allocation, you are not likely to be the market's top performer each year. To do this, you would need to put all your eggs in the single basket that performs the best in that particular year. Unfortunately this year's big winner is most often next year's big loser. Moreover, it is very difficult to predict who next year's winner will be!

Over the long haul, however, your diversified plan should be the market's best performer. While the short-term winners have a fast rise and fall, you will have your day in the sun year after year as your diversified portfolio increases its value at a consistent, steady pace.

Maximize Returns Relative To Your Risk Tolerance

There are two basic variables that will have an effect on how your portfolio is allocated: age and comfort level. Every person's financial situation is different. Each has a different approach to asset allocation, ranging from extremely conservative to aggressive.

Your age has a direct effect on how your assets should be allocated. The less time you have to accomplish your investment objective, the more conservative you should be. If you know little Johnny or Susie is going to need money for college in two years, you don't want to do anything that would jeopardize their education. If, however, your money is earmarked for retirement 30 years from now, you'd be wise to allocate a larger percentage of your money to the growth area.

Second, you need to be able to sleep at night! All the rules, investment books and counsel you receive from your financial advisors are worthless unless you can get a good night's rest. If you are a conservative investor, by all means take the conservative route to investing; shift your asset model to fit your needs.

This does not give you the excuse to simply bury your head in the sand and only buy CDs, however. You must always be vigilant and consider the rising cost of inflation.

Allocating Your Money by Percentages

The next step is to quantify all those things that go into your allocation makeup. After determining your tolerance for risk, picking your time horizon, and establishing your goals, you will need to put a certain amount of money in each of the three investment areas — cash, income and growth. You will then allocate money based on percentages in each investment area that will fulfill your objectives.

Remember, there are no hard and fast rules that state the proportion of your money that should be in any one area. The percentages allocated to each area are relative to your personal needs.

The pie charts show two examples of what an allocation might look like for 35- and 65-year-old investors. As you can see, the 35-year-old investor has more time to prepare for retirement needs, so his or her investment portfolio will require a higher percentage of its total assets to be allocated in the growth area and less in the income area.

Two Different Asset Allocations

35 Year Old

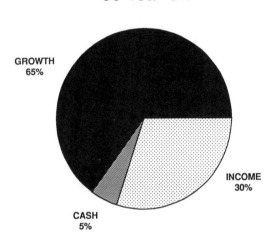

65 Year Old

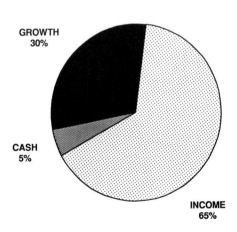

The 65-year-old investor, however, may have different needs. More specifically, he or she may want more income to live on. Then more money needs to be allocated to the income area and less to growth.

You'll notice that the allocation model *always* has some of its money allocated to growth. None of us knows for sure how long we are going to live. If you die tomorrow, it won't matter whether your assets were invested in income, growth, cash or a combination of the three. Your assets will simply be passed on to your heirs. But if you live for another 10 or 20 years, it will be very important to have your money properly allocated, so you can continue to increase your standard of living. *You can't afford to run out of money during your lifetime!*

Once you've figured out how much money you are going to need in each of the investment areas to reach proper diversification, you are going to need a *system* to monitor your portfolio. Your system will not only report your allocations, but also provide a way to move money between the investment areas as your needs change.

Your system should include *ideal* and *actual* percentages. Your ideal percentage is the portion of your money that should be allocated to each of the three investment areas (cash, income and growth) based on your objectives, time frame and risk tolerance. The actual percentage figure will show you where your money is currently allocated. These percentages sketch out the general direction in which you must move to attain proper diversification and asset allocation.

If, for example, you've become overweighted in the income area (with too much money in bonds or CDs), you will need to move some money out of income and into growth to get back to your *ideal* percentages.

You will need a reporting system to relay your current percentages for review. If changes need to be made, a strategy for moving those assets within your portfolio should be thought out beforehand to keep your costs to a minimum. A good financial consultant will have a system in place that can help you re-allocate your money as changes are made.

Final Thoughts on Asset Allocation

It is very important to incorporate asset allocation into your financial situation. You'll be surprised if you do a review of your present situation. Most people have too much money in the income area (CDs) and too little money in the growth area (stocks).

When doing a personal asset allocation analysis — as I recommend that you do — include *all* of your estate. This includes savings and checking accounts, all brokerage accounts, bank accounts (CDs) and, most importantly, your retirement savings like IRAs, annuities and retirement plans at work. As you build an allocation model that meets your needs and objectives, incorporate your retirement plans into your overall financial picture. The purpose of asset allocation is proper diversification; that includes *all* of your assets.

Finally, how often do asset allocation changes need to be made? One of the great appeals of the asset allocation strategy is that you don't have to spend a lot of time managing your assets. The asset allocation model dictates for you when changes need to be made. Ideally, changes should only be made when the system says they're necessary. It is self-regulating.

Review your situation at least once a year. This review should be fairly simple. A report will be generated showing you how each of your investments has done in the past year; it will show you where your assets stand (*actual* percentage) relative to your *ideal* percentage in each of the three investment areas. If you are more than 5% to 7% off your ideal percentages, then perhaps a change is warranted.

One last appeal of the asset allocation model is that it helps remove the emotion from investing. Most people make investment mistakes when they make hasty decisions. The allocation model will tell you to make changes only when it's to your advantage.

Chapter 8: Taxes, Inflation & Risk

Good recordkeeping has always been most people's Achilles heel. Whether you're talking about the mileage left until your car needs an oil change or what price you paid for an investment ... those who keep good, clean records make their lives much easier, especially at tax time.

This is especially important when it comes to recordkeeping in the investment world. The IRS has a one-track mind about keeping records: *It is your responsibility to keep proper records.*

When you purchase an investment — a stock, for example — you immediately create a *cost basis.* The cost basis is simply how much the security cost you when you purchased it. The cost basis for securities is normally the purchase price, including commissions paid. If you inherited the investment, your cost basis is the value on the day the previous owner died, or in some cases, six months thereafter.

The cost basis becomes important when you sell the investment. When you sell the investment, you receive a certain price for it. At that point you will either declare a loss or a gain for tax purposes.

Determining your cost basis for securities can be a difficult task if proper records are not kept. In some cases, the IRS may presume a cost basis of zero if reasonable proof is not available. But if you don't have any idea what you paid for an investment, all may not be lost. One place you can go is to old tax records. Dividends paid to you may give you an indication of the purchase date. You may also want to check with the company, which may have records of your purchase date. A third source of information is brokers. Brokers can sometimes help by sorting through old records, but there are limits to how far back they can go.

The cost basis of "gifted" stock is a little more tricky. For securities that have risen in value, the donor's cost basis and holding period become those of the recipient. For securities that have gone down in value, the cost basis to the donee will be fair market value at the date of the gift; the holding period also begins on the date of the gift.

Let's say you bought an investment years ago that has risen considerably since then, and you've decided to sell the investment. Once you've sold it (since its value has risen) you've created a *capital gain.* Capital gains are gains on investment property that is sold at a profit. If, on the other hand, you bought an investment that went down in value before you sold it, you would have a *capital loss.*

At various times, the IRS has chosen to tax capital gains at different rates depending on the holding period. In the past, if your holding period was one year or less, your capital gain or loss was considered *short-term.* If investment assets were held for more than one year, the profit or loss was considered *long-term.*

Short-term and long-term capital gains may be taxed at different rates. Because of the longstanding heated debates about legislation concerning the elimination of the capital gains tax or its rearrangement, the possibility of frequent change is high. A good tax accountant will keep abreast of the current tax laws and help you balance out your gains and losses to maximize your tax situation.

One of the significant changes in the Federal Tax Code in 1986 was the provision that allowed individuals to write off investment losses on their personal income taxes. Capital gains and losses must be netted together. If this nets a capital loss, it can be written off against ordinary income (wages from work) up to a *maximum* of $3,000 in one year. If your losses exceed the $3,000 maximum, you can carry forward the excess loss to the following year. The losses may be written off against ordinary income on a dollar-for-dollar basis.

For example, let's say you had only one trade that resulted in a $2,000 capital loss, and you had no other gains or losses. You could write off the entire $2,000 against this year's ordinary income. If, however, you had a net capital loss for the year of $5,000, you could only write off $3,000 this year. But you could write off the other $2,000 from next year's ordinary income, provided you don't have any gains next year.

If all this sounds too difficult and detailed ... you're right. It is. That's why a good tax accountant is important. He or she will help you sort through these complicated tax angles.

Some people intentionally sell an investment that has gone down in value to create a tax loss in order to offset gains. This is legal as long as you don't create a *wash sale* in the process.

A wash sale is a transaction in which the investor sells the stock at a loss and then repurchases the identical security, or options to purchase that security, within 30 days of the original sale of the stock. If the stock is repurchased within 30 days, the loss on the original sale cannot be taken as a tax loss. The 30-day period extends both before and after the sale date.

If the security is sold for a loss, the seller must wait for a minimum of 31 days before repurchasing the same or similar security for the tax loss to be recognized by the IRS.

Many investors are confused about when they have to sell their investments in order to take a gain or loss for the year. The IRS gives you until the last trading day of the year to sell a security to establish a gain or loss for the year, even though the settlement date may fall into the next year. All you need to do is to be sure that the trade date (date that you sell) is in the year you want to take the loss or gain.

Why might some people want to sell an investment this year to take a capital gain, as opposed to waiting until next year to sell the investment? One reason might be that tax rates may be rising in the following year and the investor, knowing he or she wants to sell the investment soon anyway, finds it advantageous to sell in the current year before the higher tax rates are instituted. Thus they can apply the gain to the present year's tax rates.

When you do decide to sell securities, especially shares of stock, you should specify which shares you are selling. If you have more than one position in a stock and are only selling a portion of the holdings, you can designate which position is being sold. This can make a difference in how much gain or loss you can or have to take at tax time. You will want to indicate to the brokerage firm which shares were to be sold; the confirmation will be marked accordingly.

If you cannot or do not make a specific designation of which shares are being sold, the IRS will require you to use a *first in–first out* (FIFO) method to determine which position was sold. That is, the first shares purchased are deemed to be the first shares sold. One exception is when holding shares at the brokerage firm where individual certificates cannot be specifically labeled.

Gift Tax

Some people, especially those with large estates, choose to give away some of their property or assets before they die, thereby eliminating some estate taxes. There are limits to how much an person can give away tax-free. The purpose of these limits is to prevent you from giving away all of your property before death, thereby avoiding estate taxes.

A person is allowed to give $10,000 a year away tax-free to as many individuals as he or she chooses. For example, one can give four individuals $10,000 each, every year, completely free of tax obligations. Therefore it might be advantageous for the donor to spread gifts over a period of years to take advantage of the $10,000 annual exclusion to any one person in a year.

A husband and wife may give a gift of $20,000 each year to each of their children (or anyone else) without incurring any gift tax. If the maximums are exceeded in any one given year, *the donor must pay the gift tax*, not the person receiving the gift.

Note: This law does not apply to gifts between spouses. Unlimited transfers of property or gifts may be made without incurring any tax liability.

Investment Risks

One of the most important concepts in investing is understanding *risk and reward.* In an ideal world, if you assume more risk, you should get more reward. As we all know, this isn't always the case. The reason that reward doesn't always accompany risk is that there are many different types of risk. Each acts differently, depending on its origins and how you react to it.

It's inherently difficult to define and understand how the various types of risk can affect our investments and how to deal with them. For many investors, it is much easier to ignore these risks, for they seem to make investing more complicated. While this may at first appear to be the case — as well as the easy way out — an understanding of risk's effects can only make you a more informed investor. Ironically, not only will the decision making become easier, but you will also know what your probabilities of success are.

As you well know, there is no one perfect investment. All types of investments, including CDs, have some type of risk associated with them. The key to successful investing is being able to spread your risk so that one particular investment alone cannot substantially affect the returns in your total investment portfolio. Investors in CDs in the early 1990s can testify to the substantial change in their portfolio returns as reinvestment risk has torn apart their previous high returns. Let's take a look at some of the different kinds of investment risk.

The first type of risk borne by investors may be called *default risk* or *credit risk*. Simply put, credit risk refers to the uncertainty about the future financial abilities of issuers (*i.e.*, getting your money back). The risk is that an issuer of a bond, for example, may be unable to pay interest and/or principal when due on fixed income securities. Bonds rated below investment grade (junk bonds) have a high degree of credit risk. U.S. government securities have a low degree of credit risk; that's because there's a high probability that the government will repay their debt obligations.

To prevent subjecting yourself to a high degree of credit risk, you might want to check out the credit rating of the issuer of the investment. You can do this by referencing one of the rating agencies to review what it says about the credit quality of the company. Bonds rated high will have a lower credit risk than a company that's rated lower.

Whenever you buy a stock, you are taking on the risk that your investment may go down in the future ... not necessarily because of any problem with your specific investment, but because the market as a whole has forced the price down. This type of risk is called *market (systematic) risk.*

If you owned one of the best stocks in the market and the market as a whole declined substantially, there is a high probability that your investment will follow the general direction of the market, at least in the short run. Because the market in general may temporarily pull down the value of your stock, you are assuming some market risk. The risk is that if you needed money for an emergency during this time, you would be forced to sell at a loss.

Unfortunately, there is really no way of eliminating market risk. Ultimately, your goal should be to contain the market risk within your acceptable risk parameters. You can do this by spreading out your money in different stocks whose markets move in different directions at different degrees.

A risk associated with bonds that's much like the market risk associated with stocks is *interest rate risk.* Your risk is that if interest rates rise, the price of your bonds will fall. If you needed to sell your bonds while the price had fallen, you would get less than you put in.

Not all bond prices fall to the same degree, however. A long-term (20 year maturity) bond's price will fall much farther and faster than a short-term bond such as one with a three- or four-year maturity. A short-term bond is less affected by interest rate risk. To spread your risk, you may want to own both short-term and long-term bonds.

Some stocks are also exposed and are said to be interest-rate sensitive. For example, utilities borrow money to finance operations. An increase in interest rates requires the utility company to pay more for future financing. This added expense will reduce profitability, causing the price of the stock to decline.

Why might you want to own some long-term bonds if they have a higher degree of interest-rate risk than short-term bonds? *Reinvestment risk* is the reason investors should own some longer-term income investments. The early 1990s are a testimonial to the effects of reinvestment risk. Reinvestment risk is simply the risk that someone who owns a CD or bond will be unable to reinvest at the level of interest rates that was available at the time of purchase.

In the early 1990s, investors were forced to renew their CDs at 3% and 4%, when only a couple years earlier they were earning around 9%. This risk has most directly affected retired investors who rely on the income from their bonds and CDs for living expenses. It also affects the total return on your balanced portfolio.

The way to manage reinvestment risk is to own some longer-term CDs and bonds in addition to your short-term holdings. That way if interest rates continue to fall, you will have the satisfaction of knowing some of your money will be locked in at higher rates for a longer period of time.

One of the most damaging and overlooked types of risk is *purchasing power risk* or *inflationary risk*. This risk refers to the decline of purchasing power of your money. For example, if the rate of inflation is 5% for a given year, it will take $1.05 to purchase the same item that could have been bought for $1 at the beginning of that year. Purchasing power has decreased; the dollar will not buy as much as it would previously. That means if your investment, *after taxes*, hasn't earned at least 5%, then your standard of living is not increasing, and in fact may be going down.

Inflationary risk is primarily associated with fixed-income investments like CDs and bonds. The primary risk of buying a bond or CD is that inflation will erode the purchasing power of your money when the investment matures.

For example, in 1971 a book of stamps cost $1.60. Today, that same book of stamps costs $5.80. In 1969 a $100,000 CD generated enough income to buy a brand new luxury car ($6,000) plus take a week-long cruise. Today, the same $100,000 CD doesn't generate enough income to buy one-fourth of the car ($25,000) — and forget the cruise!

You need to remember that the value of your money today will not be the same in the future.

How do you combat inflationary risk? Historically, stocks and variable annuities have provided the best protection against this type of risk, since their income tends to increase with inflation.

Good-quality utility companies with histories of steadily increasing dividends also provide an excellent hedge for investors who need their investment income to live on. Not only do the utility's dividends (income paid out to shareholders) normally increase year after year, but the value of utility companies rises over time as well.

Finally, when evaluating the merits of an investment, you must look at how easily your security may be bought and sold. This type of risk is referred to as *liquidity risk.* How marketable is the investment? Generally, the larger the issuer, the more easily you should be able to sell your investment. It may be easier to get a fair price for your investment on the New York Stock Exchange than, say, securities trading on the more thinly traded over-the-counter market.

Inflation

"A nickel ain't worth a dime anymore."
                                                    - Yogi Berra

Inflation is an investment concept that is not so much misunderstood as *ignored!* I cannot stress enough that as an investor, you must take into account the effect of inflation on your return on investments. Otherwise you are risking the chance of outliving your money or, at the very least, lowering your standard living.

Even economists can't agree on the hows and whys of inflation. The most common explanation is that inflation is caused by a money supply that expands too rapidly. This so-called *easy money* or *loose money* policy creates a situation where there's too much spending money and not enough goods and services on which to spend it all. In other words, supply is lower than demand. The result is consumers compete for limited goods; thus, prices escalate.

If inflation is defined as a rise in the general level of prices, how is it measured? This problem is easily solved when referring to the price change of one type of goods, but it becomes trickier when dealing with a larger number of goods, some with prices that have risen faster than others.

Realistically, price changes for all the goods produced by

the economy cannot be computed. Instead, statisticians for the federal government have selected a representative market basket of goods, and then compute the price changes of the market basket every month.

The consumer price index (CPI), the producer price index (PPI) and the gross domestic product (GDP) are the three price indexes that government statisticians use most often to determine the general level of inflation. Each of these indexes measures the average price change for the goods and services that comprise the index.

Inflation can seem an obscure concept unless we put its effect into real-life contexts. In 1967, a gallon of gasoline cost $.23; today that same gallon of gasoline costs $1.20. In other words, it cost $3.45 to fill your car with gas in 1967, but today it costs about $18 to fill that same tank. A one-pound steak in 1967 cost $.98; today it sells for $2.50. Can you imagine what these items will cost in another 10 or 20 years?

No one knows for sure how much effect inflation is going to have on the purchasing power of our money in the future, but it is important that we prepare ahead of time for these highly probable price increases. As Will Rogers once said, "Invest in inflation. It's the only thing going up."

We've all seen the effects of the cost of our electric and heating bills go up almost yearly. What can we do? Investors need to create a balanced portfolio that will provide returns that will combat the *thief* called inflation.

Most importantly, investors need to factor in the effect of inflation on their portfolio return to see if their *real rate of return* is positive. The real rate of return is your return after taxes and inflation. If your real rate of return is positive, then your standard of living is going up and the value of your money (purchasing power) is staying ahead of inflation.

Here's an example of how you go about calculating the real rate of return. You need to subtract your current taxes and the annual inflation rate from your investment's return to get your real rate of return. For example,

Portfolio total return	*10.0%*
– minus taxes (28% rate)	*2.8%*
– minus inflation rate	*5.0%*
= your real rate of return	*+2.2%*

In this case your *true return* or real rate of return is +2.2% after taxes and inflation. In other words, the value of your money has truly risen 2% more than the average prices you paid for goods that year. Thus, your standard of living has increased.

However, a much different scenario occurred in the late '70s and early '80s. Let's look at the real rates of return earned by CD owners in 1979 who were earning 11.4% that year. It sounded pretty good, right? Let's take a look.

CD interest rate (1979)	*11.4%*
–minus taxes (59%, top rate)	*6.7%*
–minus inflation rate (1979)	*13.0%*
= your real rate of return	*– 8.3%*

As you can see, earning a high rate of return doesn't automatically mean you really are making money. Your true rate of return is relative to the taxes you pay and the current inflation rate. Earning a low rate of investment return may not necessarily be bad as long as the rate of inflation is also low. It is possible to earn 5% on your money and still have a real rate of return that is better than those who earned 10% to 15% in the early 1980s with high inflation!

Ultimately your goal is not necessarily to earn a high rate of return, but rather to earn a rate of return that is positive after taxes and inflation. A reasonable goal might be to earn a real rate of return of perhaps 2% to 3% per year.

If you are in the 28% tax bracket and assume an average inflation rate of 4%, your investments need to return almost 6% to maintain your current purchasing power (break even) after taxes and inflation. To earn a net real return of 2%, given these factors, you must earn 8½% overall on your investments.

However, inflation is not necessarily bad for everyone. It's good for debtors (people who borrow money). In inflationary times, it's much easier to earn the $1,000 you need to pay back a loan taken out five years ago. What you actually pay back in *real* terms is much less that $1,000, since the money you use to repay the lender won't buy nearly what it would have bought five years before.

The buying power of the dollar declined dramatically

during the inflation-ravaged years of the early 1980s. To
many, inflation seemed a way of life that would never end.
But, of course, its rapid pace did slow. The result is lower
interest rates.

According to the U.S. Bureau of Labor Statistics Consumer
Price Index, the annual inflation rates (CPI) between December
31, 1925, and December 31,1992, are as follows:

1 year	2.98%
5 years	4.24%
10 years	3.82%
20 years	6.22%
50 years	4.35%
65 years	3.29%

Chapter 9: Re-evaluating 'Risk'

Don't Run Out of Money
Before Running Out of Life

Risk is one of the most widely used concepts investors rely on to determine whether or not to buy an investment. Unfortunately, some investors' definition of risk may not be exactly accurate depending on the person's understanding of what risk really is.

For many people, the basic understanding of "risk" and "safety" comes from the Great Depression — a massive period of deflation during which most lost their principal. It didn't matter whether one was an investor in New York City who owned a piece of Fifth Avenue and a portfolio of common stocks or a farmer in North Dakota who owned farmland and machinery; at the depression's end, the value of most things had gone down. This loss of principal is the understanding of risk that, if we didn't experience directly, our parents and grandparents taught us.

How do you define "risk"? Yes, principal loss is a risk, and a risk not to be taken lightly. But have you ever considered that there might be other risks in your life-some even more real than the risk of losing one's principal? How about the risk that your retirement income won't keep up with the rising costs of living. As we retire much sooner and live much longer, even very low levels of inflation are going to turn our dollars into pennies over time. In 1976 a stamp cost 13 cents; in 1996 that same stamp costs 32 cents. The longer you live, the bigger this risk becomes.

How do you define "safety"? Most people would respond with just the opposite of risk; *keeping* one's principal safe. But safe from what? Safe from the rising costs of living? It is very easy to keep your principal from fluctuating by buying CDs. But because your principal can never grow, you have exposed your money, in my opinion, to the greatest financial risk of all; erosion of purchasing power. With fixed income investments (CDs and bonds) you can only get back, at maturity, what you put in. But, because of the rising costs of living, what you put in five or 10 years ago will not buy as much 10 or 20 years in the future. In the real world of persistent inflation, putting all of your money in fixed income investments is not very safe at all.

Thirty years ago, our parents or grandparents often retired at 65 and died at 72. The idea of risk of principal was more realistic than today. Today people are living a lot longer. The average person is living a quarter of a century after retirement, and he or she continues to invest most of his or her money in fixed income investments like CDs and Government bonds whose principal and interest never grow. This obsession with principal can be financially devastating to people today.

In the first half of the 20th century, most people worked for a company until retirement, then lived off their retirement savings until death. Their life expectancy was significantly shorter than today's. People were able to take their retirement savings and live off the income until they died. Life expectancy was shorter so they required less money to live. The rising costs of living didn't affect as many people back then.

Today, things are different. We are living much longer into our retirement years. The average 60-year-old has a life expectancy of 21 years. It is normal today to see people living 20 to 30 years or more in retirement! It is easy to see that if a person needs to live off his or her retirement savings, those savings are going to need to grow for a long, long time. Inflation, or the cost of living, is a very big threat for today's and tomorrow's retirees.

Risk has changed because life has changed. Not only are people living longer, but since the Great Depression, our country has not seen another decade in which prices have fallen. During every decade since the Depression, the costs of the things we buy have gone up.

The primary risk for people today, and in the 21st century, is erosion of purchasing power, that is, outliving one's income.

I don't mean literally running out of money, although that is a possibility. I mean the *risk of the income one lives on from year-to-year not keeping up with the perpetual rise in the cost of the goods and services a person buys.*

Let's say someone is getting a fixed income of $2,000 a month from his or her CDs, bonds and other savings. Sounds okay today, right? How about getting $2,000 a month for the next 21 years? Remember, the cost of the things you buy are going to go up virtually every year. If your income doesn't rise along with prices, you may eventually outlive your fixed retirement income. The cost of a 1972 stamp was six cents; today it is 32 cents. If your investments were returning six cents in 1972, are they returning at least 32 cents today?

Someone might ask himself, "Will $24,000 a year today buy as many things as $24,000 a year 10 or 20 years from now?" Obviously not! For example, with an average annual inflation rate of 3.5% for the next 21 years, that $24,000 annual income 21 years from now, would be worth only about $12,000 in today's dollars. Assuming one is used to living on $24,000 annually, he must ask himself, "Can I afford to cut my income in half?" If the answer is "no" and he can't afford to live on less, then it is important that he get his income to go up for the rest of his life to keep up with the rising costs of living. Given an annual inflation rate of 3.5%, one's annual income needs to grow to about $48,000 by the 21st year to keep the standard of living the same as today's $24,000 per year.

So how can one achieve rising income to offset the increasing cost of living? By receiving the *dividends* that the great companies in America pay on their common stocks. Many of these companies have been raising the dividends they pay for many, many years. One of the most convenient ways to own those great businesses is by buying a good quality mutual fund or variable annuity with a *long track record of rising dividends.* Investments like these should help keep one's income rising throughout one's life.

Fluctuation Is NOT Loss

What do people like least about owning a basket of common stocks of America's great companies? The *fluctuation!* This is the stumbling block that keeps a lot of people from owning and staying with this great investment.

Please understand that *fluctuation is not loss,* unless you choose to make it so with a panicky sell decision. The value of the shares of the great companies in America and around the world are going to fluctuate; up mostly, but never mind that. Every once in a while their share prices will go down. But they never stay down. Every time the stock market went down it ultimately recovered and moved on to new highs.

You see, all investments have a cost and benefit. In *savings* (CDs, Treasury bills, savings accounts, money markets) the benefit is that you know exactly how many dollars you have today and how many you will have tomorrow. Your principal stays virtually constant all the time. There is great emotional comfort in this.

The cost of emotional comfort in savings is that your returns are almost always negative after factoring in taxes and inflation. In other words, your dollars are losing value relative to what you can buy with that money. The stamp you paid 32 cents for in 1996, used to cost 13 cents in 1976. The price of everything you need to live on is constantly rising and that means that the value of your dollars are declining.

In *investing* (common stocks), your money has a different cost and benefit. The *cost* of investing is that your principal is going to fluctuate, mostly upward. The Dow Jones Industrial Average touched 40 in 1932; in 1995 it surpassed 5,000! I can assure you that there were many periods of time during which the market declined during those years. Some of those periods lasted longer than others. But the share prices of these companies never stayed down. The declines have been temporary. What's been the great risk of that period? I would say that the great risk was not owning these companies' common stocks.

The *benefit* of investing is that your money, over time, will likely keep ahead of inflation and taxes. No other investment has more reliably provided investors with positive real rates of return than common stocks and the dividends they pay. The cost of this benefit is temporary; it's fluctuation. And fluctuation is not loss; it's fluctuation. The benefit is permanent; over time, your income will grow faster than the rising costs of living.

Remember, risk is not just loss of principal. That's one risk, and can never again be the only risk. Another risk for people today and in the future, perhaps more important, is loss of purchasing power. You cannot afford to run out of money during your lifetime!

Chapter 10: R$_X$ for Risk: Dividend Growth

One of my beliefs for investing into the next century is that the biggest risk people will face in their financial future is *not* losing your money but "outliving it." I believe that outliving one's income is the greatest single financial risk people will face from here into the 21st century. Unlike our parents and grandparents who lived a shorter lifespan, people today, and in the future, will likely be living another 25 to 30 years in their retirement.

Not only will retirees need income for a long, long time; but they will also need *income that goes up* during their retirement years. The cost of living has gone up every decade since the Great Depression. If your income doesn't rise with the increasing costs of living, your standard of living will be declining. Remember the six-cent stamp in 1972? Today, in 1996, that same stamp costs 32 cents. Has your income from your investments risen from six cents to 32 cents over the last 24 years?

People who plan for 25 to 30 years of retirement should have an investment goal of not "growth" or "income" but, "growth *of*income." Historically, no income stream has grown more steadily and reliably than the dividends that America's great companies pay. If you believe that most companies like Coca-Cola, 3M, AT&T, McDonald's, Campbell's soup, General Electric, Mobil Oil and others will continue to sell their products and make money over time, then you should feel very comfortable with the dividends these companies will pay in the future.

Defining Dividends (The Great Inflation Killer)

Dividends are to stocks what interest is to bonds. However, the interest you earn from a stock is called a *dividend*. A dividend is a payment of cash to the shareholder of a common stock of a company. As a company makes money, they pay out some of their earnings in the form of a dividend to the shareholder.

Not all companies pay a dividend. The companies that normally pay dividends are the more mature, well-known type. Smaller or fast-growing companies normally retain their earnings so they can expand and make their company grow without having to borrow even more money from banks and others.

Let me give you a simplified example of how and where a dividend comes from. Let's assume company X makes $1 million in earnings this year. Let's also assume that there are 1 million shares of common stock held by investors. That means for every share available (1 million) there was $1 profit per share (1 million shares) — right? Right. So if a company were to be prudent, it wouldn't want to pay out all its profits to the shareholders; it may need some of that money to pay for expenses and unexpected emergencies. So most companies choose to retain some of their earnings each year.

Conversely, why don't some companies retain all of their earnings? Because they don't need all that money to run their businesses. If they aren't expanding as much anymore, they may not need that money, so they choose to reward the shareholders of the company in the form of a dividend.

Let's say that company X will retain 50% of its earnings and pay out 50% in the form of a cash dividend; it will keep those percentages fixed each year. Since company X has 1 million shares and $1 million in earnings, each share had earnings of $1. So what would the dividend be for each share? Right! Fifty cents per share (50% of $1). So if you owned 1,000 shares, your dividend would be $500 (1,000 shares x 50 cents).

Now, here is where the rising income comes in. Let's assume that company X makes $1,200,000 next year. What would happen to your dividend income next year? Well, if the company's payout ratio stays the same at 50/50, then 50% of $1,200,000 is $600,000. If you still own 1,000 shares of company X, your dividend income would be $600! You see, your income has risen from $500 to $600. As these companies' earnings increase, shareholders are rewarded for their patience and long term perspective. The form of that reward: increased dividends, the ultimate inflation killer.

But that's not the whole story yet. If a company keeps increasing its earnings year after year, and its dividends keep growing along with earnings, it just makes sense that the price of the shares of that company would eventually go up as well. Why? Because the shares become more valuable as the dividend rises.

It is impossible for the price of a stock and the dividend to go in opposite directions for any length of time. Dividend growth signals, in the most concrete way, that a company is doing progressively better. If the company is doing better over time, the price of the stock may go down once in a while, but it cannot stay down. Ultimately the value of the shares will rise over time. So not only can you achieve rising income, but your principal can grow also. That is the ultimate inflation killer.

Let's look at a case for rising income: Coca-Cola Co. A $10,000 investment in Coca-Cola stock at the end of 1983 would have purchased 2,243 shares, adjusted for splits. Each share paid a dividend of .23 cents in 1984. The income from these shares was $516 (2,243 x .23) in 1984, for a yield of 5.16%. The following graph illustrates how Coca-Cola's dividend income has grown over the past 10 years. Keep in mind, the income in this illustration is shown as being paid out to the shareholder to use to live on to pay bills etc. The share value (principal) is growing without dividends being reinvested.

Coca-Cola Co.

Year	Dividend per share	Income	Yield on original investment	Principal value
1984	$.23	$516	5.16%	$11,569
1985	$.25	$561	5.61%	$15,794
1986	$.26	$583	5.83%	$21,170
1987	$.28	$628	6.28%	$21,381
1988	$.30	$673	6.73%	$25,026
1989	$.34	$763	7.63%	$43,322
1990	$.40	$897	8.97%	$52,155
1991	$.48	$1,077	10.77%	$90,009
1992	$.56	$1,256	12.56%	$93,935
1993	$.68	$1,525	15.25%	$100,103

As you can readily see, in the last ten years, Coca-Cola Co. has paid a very consistent rising dividend that ultimately offset the increasing costs of living. Not only did the income rise consistently, but the share value grew as well. Remember the income was not reinvested. As Coca-Cola's dividend rose over the years, their shares became more valuable and hence Coca-Cola's share price increased. Long-term *dividend* growth is a sure sign that a company is doing progressively better and over time the price of the shares of that company will go up.

Does all this sound to good to be true? Allow me to share just a few other companies' dividend growth patterns.

Dividend Growth Patterns

Company	Cash Dividend		Yield of Dividend on Original Investment	
	1984	1993	1984	1993
Bristol Meyers Squibb	$.80	$2.88	3.78%	13.62%
Exxon	$1.68	$2.88	8.99%	15.41%
Campbell Soup	$.28	$.92	3.67%	12.06%
Colgate-Palmolive	$.64	$1.34	5.95%	12.46%
Gillette	$.31	$.81	5.10%	13.32%
Pepsico	$.19	$.61	4.47%	14.35%
Sara Lee	$.16	$.56	4.92%	17.23%

As you can see, the shares of these companies can provide investors with substantial rising income. Historically, owning these great companies has been the only way to keep your principal and income growing faster than inflation and taxes. It makes sense then that most people should have some of their money in these companies to achieve rising income.

What is the easiest and most convenient way to own these companies? In my opinion, investors should buy shares in mutual funds and variable annuities that own these great businesses. That way you won't have to worry about when to buy or sell or what company to pick. The mutual fund manager will do all that for you. All you have to do is sit back and collect those dividend checks when you need them.

So how do you know which mutual fund to buy shares in? That's the job of your financial advisor. Because there are more than 5,000 mutual funds to pick from, it has become very complicated. Many mutual funds pay little or no dividend at all, and most have no long-term proven track record. You shouldn't go out and blindly buy a stock mutual fund thinking it owns the companies that pay rising dividends. Most do not.

If you are a long-term investor who plans on living a long time in retirement, dividends might just be the answer to your rising income needs. None of us know for sure how long we are going to live. So if we do live a long time in retirement, dividends should help keep our standard of living rising throughout our golden years.

Chapter 11: Getting Started

Selecting a Financial Consultant

How do you find a financial consultant whose advice you can trust? Back in the bullish periods of the 1980s, it almost didn't matter whether your financial consultant was a genius, a rocket scientist, or simply somebody's smiling son-in-law. If you had money in the markets in the 1980s, you were almost assured of making money.

That's not true in today's fluctuating markets. With the huge array of new investments available, coupled with the barrage of men and women entering the financial services industry, it is important to find a financial consultant who has the ability to communicate with you to help you truly understand the complexities of various investments and asset allocations.

Choosing the right financial consultant is not quite as important as selecting the right spouse ... but since the consultant will do much to determine if you are financially comfortable in the future, it is a decision to be taken seriously.

One possible source for finding a financial consultant may be referrals from your friends or colleagues. It is important, though, for you to do your homework, even with referrals from your friends. You need to interview the person they've recommended to get a feel for the way he or she does business.

If you aren't comfortable asking a friend or coworker for a referral, and you haven't come in social contact with a financial consultant, you may need to go out and visit with some of the brokerage firms in your city.

You might start by looking in the Yellow Pages under "Stock & Bond Brokers" or "Investment Securities." Call the offices and ask to speak with one of their financial consultants; then set up an interview appointment. Remember, this is a two-way interview. Not only should the consultant be asking you some questions; most important, you must interview the consultant to see if you feel comfortable trusting this person with your money.

If you are starting out cold, not knowing a soul, you should interview more than merely one potential consultant ... perhaps two or three. This may give you a better perspective on who you think can do the best job managing your money.

When you sit down with a prospective financial consultant be sure to *ask questions*. Ask: How long has he or she been a financial consultant? Where does he or she get information? What is his or her track record? How does he or she track and communicate how clients' accounts are doing? What is his or her reporting method? Ask for some statistics regarding past successes or failures.

Most important, ask the financial consultant what his or her *investment philosophy* is. Is he or she simply shooting from the hip, or is there a deeper reason for the recommendations? Does this philosophy make sense to you?

Your financial consultant's investment *philosophy* separates the qualified from the non-qualified. Your consultant's philosophy should mirror your feelings toward investing. If your philosophy is long-term buy and hold and the prospective financial consultant prefers to take quick profits, you'd be well off looking for someone else.

You should expect the consultant to create and explain an investment plan, or system, that directly meets your needs, not simply pass on the latest hot stock or investment idea. The investment plan should include some type of philosophy on asset allocation and strategy to deal with profits and losses.

Your advisor should be inquisitive and ask you a lot of in-depth questions. This person is going to need to know a lot about you. If you're truly serious about getting advice from a financial consultant, it is important that you share not only all of your financial information but your true feelings toward investing: investment preferences, risk tolerances, priorities, values and goals. Without this information, it is impossible to get informed advice from a financial consultant. If he or she doesn't ask much about you and your feelings about investing, you might consider shopping around for another perspective.

Once you have described your situation and goals to the financial consultant, listen to his or her reaction and comments. Do they make sense? Can you understand the recommendations or perspectives? Just because you've taken time to listen to his or her recommendations doesn't mean you have to invest. But if you feel comfortable with his or her philosophy and recommendations, don't procrastinate. Remember, there is no bad time to make a good investment!

One way financial consultants get new clients is by "cold calling" on the telephone. If you have an interest in listening to their idea over the telephone, go ahead. But you are not obligated to listen. You may choose to end the phone conversation at any time.

Personally, I think it's worthwhile to meet a financial consultant *face to face* before doing business. You are establishing a relationship that will directly affect your future. It might be a little inconvenient to arrange the meeting, but after all, it's your money we're talking about!

The most important thing you should expect from a financial consultant is *honesty.* It is important that he or she not only communicates to you when the market is up, but also takes time to explain why your particular investment is down. You should expect the financial consultant to keep you informed regularly, in good times and bad. If you feel uncomfortable with the way your account is being handled, it's your responsibility to take the initiative to make a change.

Your financial consultant should be up front about how he or she is paid. You can ask how the financial consultant is compensated. If he or she seems hesitant to offer that information or tries to hide the fees or commissions, you may be dealing with someone who is less than honest, with not necessarily your best interest at heart.

A good financial consultant will be worth far more than what you pay in commissions. Remember, fees and commissions are how financial consultants get paid. There is more to successful investing than simply picking good investments. A good financial consultant will be able to fuse together the many different aspects of estate planning such as investments, insurance and tax planning.

How Do I Get Started?

As a general rule, regardless of your age, the first thing you need to accomplish is to build up a cash account that will serve as an emergency fund for the future. The amount you should keep in this money market depends on your individual needs. Some people need more money readily available than others. Keep enough money available to give you peace of mind.

If you have children in school, knowing they could need money at any time, it would be wise to keep a larger balance available. Likewise, if you or a dependent are in poor health, a larger emergency fund would be appropriate.

Many people overdo it when it comes to "keeping their powder dry." If you need cash and have your funds invested in good stocks, mutual funds and so on, you can usually sell whenever you desire. But since you're never sure what they will be worth at any given time, you may not want to sell.

To maximize your returns, don't keep a lot of money sitting idle waiting for that emergency to come along. If you need temporary money, you can borrow against your investments; that way, you can rent a lot of time waiting for your emergency. Because you can borrow against your own account, you essentially have cash available at any time, while still remaining fully invested.

Once you achieved your desired level of savings in your emergency fund, decide *how* you are going to invest. If you are starting out with lesser amounts of money, you are probably best off starting out putting some money in a mutual fund.

Your next decision — which one? If you choose a no-load mutual fund, you need to start doing your own research. After deciding on a particular fund that specifically meets your needs relative to risk and reward, you must call the mutual fund family to begin the paperwork process. Once you've received the applications, you would need to fill them out and send them your money. They will provide you with confirmations and statements regarding the status of your fund or funds.

If you choose to get advice from a financial consultant, you first job is to find a consultant you're comfortable with. Once you've accomplished that, the financial consultant will take care of setting up the account and guiding you through the investment process. Your financial consultant will be able to give you advice on which fund best fits your needs relative to your total financial picture.

Once you've accumulated some money into a fund or number of funds, you can choose to diversify by buying individual stocks or bonds. To buy these securities, you must go through a broker/dealer. You can do this two ways: through a *full-service* brokerage firm or a *discount* broker.

If you make all your own decisions, perform your own research and don't want or need any advice, then perhaps a discount brokerage best fits your needs. Discount brokerage firms do not offer many services of full-service brokerages. They will not send you research or suggest a price at which to buy or sell your stock. But they will charge you a lower commission rate than full-service brokerage firms. The commissions usually vary with the size and volume of trading that you do.

If you are fairly new at investing and don't know your way around Wall Street, a traditional full-service brokerage firm is the right choice for you. A financial consultant will advise you on what to buy, what to sell, and when to buy or sell.

When trying to determine how to start out the investment process, do not underestimate the pressures of investing on your own. When the market is fluctuating, or your investment is moving in the right or wrong direction, you will have no resource to help you make any decisions. The stamina of your stomach and your ability to rest at night — knowing you need to make all your own decissions — should weigh heavily when deciding whether you should go it alone or seek advice.

Establishing Your Brokerage Account

Opening an account with a financial consultant can be as easy as opening a checking account at a bank. You will need to provide basic personal information as well as financial information such as your assets, your tax bracket, your financial objectives and any questions you may have.

Once your account has been opened, you can make a

purchase or sale. A confirmation will be sent to you showing you the transaction you made. It will show the commission and fees, net amount due, the price you paid for the investment and other information.

After your account has been opened, you may place buy and sell orders by telephone with your financial consultant and he or she will send a confirmation showing you exactly how much you owe.

Common Investment Mistakes and How to Avoid Them

Even the best-educated, most well-informed investors make mistakes from time to time. It is important that we learn from our predecessors so we don't make the same mistakes they did!

Two of the most common-sense principles of successful investing are *patience and discipline.* Patience means understanding that the best investment results are achieved over time, rather than immediately. Discipline refers to the ability to stay focused on the long view, especially when those around you are preoccupied with riskier short-term results.

I've compiled a checklist of common investment mistakes most often made by the average investor. By understanding these pitfalls, we can invest our savings more efficiently and avoid wasting as much money as those who have gone before us.

Investing Too Conservatively

A common mistake is to invest your savings too conservatively, especially during your working years when asset accumulation and growth are most important. Many investors erroneously believe that they cannot take any risk whatsoever when it comes to their savings and retirement. As a result, they invest most or all of their money in safe but low-yielding money markets and CDs. Investing too conservatively always risks losing purchasing power, because investment returns simply do not keep up with the increasing cost of living (inflation).

If your current investment portfolio doesn't have a portion of securities that will rise with inflation, it is important that you add some protection like stocks or stock mutual funds. You don't have to do it all at once, but investing for inflation protection should be a major concern and you need to position your assets accordingly.

Chasing High Yields

The yields on interest-earning investments can rise and fall dramatically as interest rates work through their cycles. A common mistake, especially for retired investors who rely on fixed income, is buying investments that offer the highest yield. To get a higher yield, investors are unknowingly assuming more risk to get these higher returns. Remember, *the higher the yield, the higher the risk.*

Don't blindly chase for the highest yields. Shop around for returns that appear to be consistent with today's interest rate market. If you do decide to look around for a "higher yield", make sure you have defined the risk level you are willing to assume to achieve that yield, and don't chase beyond that risk tolerance.

Inappropriate Investments

Because investors and uninformed salespeople who market investments chase yields and returns, some investors have purchased securities that are not appropriate for their individual needs. Many investments have a higher of risk level than uninformed salespeople and investors are aware of. Consequently, undue risk is assumed by the owner of the investment.

It is important that you stick with investments that you understand. Understanding how an investment works and why it's appropriate are great questions to ask. If you don't get a satisfactory explanation that makes sense to you within a couple of sentences, you may want to step back and reconsider. *The best investments are the investments that meet your unique individual needs.*

Maintain Too Many Accounts

Some investors have opened many brokerage accounts. Outside of the obvious complexity of tax-time considerations, maintaining more than one brokerage account most often leads to excess fees as well as headaches.

You might feel apprehensive when making an investment decision because you may get conflicting opinions from two different financial consultants. In addition to different education levels, neither consultant may be aware of the other's account; thus, neither can truly give you informed advice regarding your investment decision. No wonder their advice seems to conflict!

If you have a number of accounts, consolidate them and make your life easier. But before you do this, find a financial consultant with whom you feel comfortable and trust. Build a long-term, trusting relationship with this person. In the long run, it will be well worth your time.

Unrealistic Expectations

In the world of investments, it takes patience and discipline to build wealth. Too many investors expect to get rich quick, demanding dramatic and immediate returns from their investments. These people are always disappointed when their expectations are not met.

The decade of the 1980s was quite remarkable for investors. The stock and bond markets did exceptionally well. That decade will be a hard act to follow. No one can tell what the next ten years will bring to investment returns, but a look at history may offer an idea of what you can reasonably expect.

Take a look at the past 25 or 50 years to determine what you might expect on your investments. Then give them time to compound and grow. Remember, six months to two years is not a reasonable period of time to measure your investments' returns if you are truly a long-term investor.

I'm not suggesting that you avoid considering changes in your portfolio if they are warranted in the short term. But don't become discouraged if an investment hasn't met your long-term expectations in a shorter period of time. You need to invest time along with your money.

Chapter 12: Finally ...

There are three things I feel certain about concerning the next 25 years.

One: Your cost of living will go up substantially. It is very important that you recognize this fact. Inflation is going to eat away at the value of your money.

Two: The government is going to tax you as much as it can for as long as you live.

Three: The stock and bond markets should do very well over the long term. Over the next decade, some 75 million American baby boomers, now in the 30- to 40-year-old age brackets, will be passing through the time in their lives when people invariably spend the most for houses, cars, books, medical care, clothing and education for themselves and their children.

How much will the stock market go up? When will it fall? Where will the stock market be in six months or at this time two years from now? Where will interest rates be?

I do not know — and I do not know anyone who does.

I am certain that at some point the market will temporarily decline as it always has in the past. I do not believe that it matters very much, because almost all of us should be looking at the market from a long-term point of view.

I believe the market and the economy will be much higher in the future than they are today. The giant bulge in future demand from the baby boom generation will not go away.

Now that you've studied everything from CDs to stocks, it is time to put this knowledge to work. As you build and maintain your future estate, remember that *time in the market* is much more important than *timing in the market*. If you take a long-term perspective, maintain reasonable expectations for your money, and allocate your money so you achieve the safety of income with the rewards of growth, you will most certainly accomplish your goals.

About the Author

Dan Geffre is a financial advisor with a national brokerage firm. A graduate of Moorhead (Minn.) State University, he acquired advanced business training in Louisiana and North Carolina before joining his firm in Fargo, North Dakota. He is a licensed New York Stock Exchange stockbroker. Dan holds several licenses in insurance, including life, health and annuity, and is a member of the Red River Estate Planning Council. He is a candidate for a master's degree in financial services from the American College, Bryn Mawr, Pennsylvania. Dan shares his wide experience in financial planning through seminars and adult education classes throughout the region.

If you are interested in Dan's educational seminars or classes, or if you have any comments, please write:

> ***Any Questions?***
> **P.O. Box 9872**
> **Fargo, N.D. 58106–9872**